WOK

cooking MADE EASY

Delicious Meals in Minutes

by Nongkran Daks, Alexandra Greeley, Rohani Jelani,
Chef Tummanoon Punchun, Daniel Reid,
Devagi Sanmugam and Cecilia Au-Yang

With easy to follow, step-by-step instructions,
this book shows you how to combine the
health benefits of wok and stir-fry cooking with all the
unique flavors of Asia. Included here are over 65 quick and
delicious recipes prepared with a wok.

PERIPLUS EDITIONS
Singapore • Hong Kong • Indonesia

Contents

MAIL ORDER SOURCES

Finding the ingredients for Asian home cooking has become very simple. Most supermarkets carry staples such as soy sauce, fresh ginger, and fresh lemongrass. Almost every large metropolitan area has Asian markets serving the local population—just check your local business directory. With the Internet, exotic Asian ingredients and cooking utensils can be easily found online. The following list is a good starting point of online merchants offering a wide variety of goods and services.

http://www.asiafoods.com
http://www.geocities.com/MadisonAvenue/8074/VarorE.html
http://dmoz.org/Shopping/Food/Ethnic_and_Regional/Asian/
http://templeofthai.com/
http://www.orientalpantry.com/
http://www.zestyfoods.com/
http://www.thaigrocer.com/Merchant/index.htm
http://asianwok.com/
http://pilipinomart.com/
http://www.indiangrocerynet.com/
http://www.orientalfoodexpress.com/

Mention "wok cooking," and one immediately visualizes a huge wok being wielded above a mighty flame by an Asian chef. One also thinks Asian "comfort food"—with accompanying images of wholesome and thoughtfully prepared meals, eaten together with family members in the comfort of the home.

While there is sometimes still a mystique that Asian chefs meticulously prepare all their ingredients in the elaborate ancestral manner, the truth is that many home chefs in Asia today can now hardly afford the time to do so. But fortunately, wok stir-frying is one of the best and quickest cooking methods to use. Because of the intense heat required, the food is cooked rapidly, and its taste and nutritional value are preserved. The Chinese wok is a fantastic implement, as its deep bowl-like shape and sloping sides ensure that the ingredients remain in the center, where the heat is most intense.

The aim of *Wok Cooking Made Easy* is to introduce nutritious and easy-to-prepare Asian wok recipes to a Western audience—ranging from a simple Spinach with Garlic stir-fry to Hot and Spicy Sichuan Tofu, Sliced Fish with Mushrooms and Ginger, and the classic Sichuan Chicken with Dried Chilies, Thai Fried Rice and Five Spice Chicken.

All of the recipes in this volume are light, healthy and tasty and require no special skills to prepare. May this book bring endless cooking pleasure as you venture into the world of Asian cuisine.

Important Asian Ingredients

Asian eggplants are long and slender, smaller and slightly milder than Mediterranean globe eggplants. Asian eggplants can be either purple or green.

Bean paste is made from fermented black or yellow soybeans, and is an important seasoning in Asian dishes. **Black bean paste** (**tau cheo**) has a strong, salty flavor, while **yellow bean paste** (**miso**) is slightly sweet. "Sweet" and "hot" salted beans have added sugar or garlic and chili. Soybean pastes are available at Asian food stores.

Black Chinese mushrooms, also known as shiitake mushrooms, are used widely in Asian cooking. The dried ones must be soaked in hot water to soften before use, from 15 minutes to an hour, depending on the thickness. The stems are removed and discarded; only the caps are used. Fresh shiitake mushroom stems can be eaten if the bottoms are trimmed.

Cardamom pods are highly aromatic and contain tiny black seeds. If whole pods are used, they should be removed from the food before serving. If only the seeds are called for, lightly smash the pods and remove the seeds, discarding the pods. Ground cardamon is sold in packets or tins.

Dried red
finger-length chilies

Bird's-eye chilies

Fresh red finger-length chilies

Chili peppers come in many shapes, sizes and colors. Fresh green and red Asian **finger-length chilies** are moderately hot. Tiny red, green or orange **bird's-eye chilies** (*chili padi*) are very hot. **Dried chilies** are usually deseeded, cut into lengths and soaked in warm water to soften before use. **Ground red pepper,** also known as **cayenne** is made from ground dried chilies. **Chili oil** is made from dried chilies or chili powder infused in oil, which is used to enliven some Sichuan dishes. **Chili paste** consists of pounded fresh or dried chilies, sometimes mixed with vinegar and garlic and sold in jars. Sichuan chili paste is made from dried chilies, soaked and ground with a touch of oil. **Chili sauce** is made by mixing ground chilies with water and seasoning the mixture with salt, sugar and vinegar or lime juice. It is available bottled and in jars.

Coconut milk is obtain by squeezing the flesh of freshly grated coconuts. To obtain **thick coconut milk,** add 1 cup (250 ml) of water to the grated flesh of one coconut, then squeeze and strain. Although freshly squeezed milk has more flavor, it is now widely sold canned and in packets. **Grated fresh coconut** can be purchased from Asian markets or you can grate it yourself. Purchase coconuts that are heavy and have a lot of juice in them. Crack the coconut open and drain the juice. Break the shell into smaller pieces by turning over on a firm surface and knocking with a mallet. Use a knife to release the meat from the shell. Remove the flesh from the shell and peel the brown outer skin using a vegetable peeler. Grate the flesh in a blender or food processor, adding a bit of water to help the blades turn.

Coriander is an indispensable herb and spice in Asian cooking. **Coriander seeds** are roasted and then ground in spice pastes. **Coriander roots** are used in the same way, while **coriander leaves** (also known as cilantro or Chinese parsley) are used as a herb and a garnish.

Curry powder is a spice blend that generally includes cumin seeds, coriander seeds, turmeric root, ginger root, cinnamon bark and cloves. Different spice combinations vary in color and flavor. They are sold for various types of curries—meat, fish or chicken. Use an all-purpose blend if a specific curry powder is not available.

Dried shrimp paste, also known as *belachan* is a dense mixture of fermented ground shrimp that must be toasted before use—either wrapped in foil and dry-roasted or toasted over a gas flame on the tip of a metal skewer or back of a spoon.

Fennel seeds look like

cumin seeds but are larger and paler. They add a sweet fragrance to Indian dishes, with a flavor similar to liquorice or anise. The seeds are used whole or ground.

Fish sauce is made from salted, fermented fish or shrimp. Good quality fish sauce is golden-brown in color and has a salty tang. It is available in bottles in most supermarkets.

Five Spice Powder is a highly aromatic blend of Sichuan pepper, cinnamon, clove, fennel and star anise, ground to a fine powder.

Galangal is similar in appearance to ginger and a member of the same family. This aromatic root has a distinctive flavor that is used in dishes throughout Asia. Dried galangal lacks the fragrance of fresh galangal, so try to buy it fresh. It can be sliced and kept sealed in the freezer for several months.

Garlic chives or *gu cai,* also known as Chinese chives, have long, green flat leaves that resemble thin green onions. They have a strong garlicky flavor and are often added to noodle or stir-fried vegetable dishes during the final stages of cooking. If you cannot get them, use green onions or regular chives instead.

Green onions, also known as scallions, have slender stalks with dark green leaves and white bases. They are sliced and sprinkled generously on soups and other dishes as a garnish.

Kaffir lime leaves are used in soups and curries of Thai, Malay or Indonesian origin. They are also thinly sliced and used as a garnish. Buy them fresh, frozen or dried—fresh or frozen leaves are much more fragrant.

Lemongrass is a highly aromatic herb stalk. The tough outer layers of the stem should be peeled away and only the pale, inner flesh of the thick lower part of the stalk is used.

Mustard seeds are small brownish-black seeds that are commonly used in Indian cooking, imparting a nutty flavor to dishes.

Fresh yellow wheat noodles (mee)

Dried rice vermicelli (*beehoon*)

flat rice noodles (*kway teow*)

Noodles are a universal favorite in Asia. Both fresh and dried noodles are made from either wheat, rice or mung bean flour. **Fresh yellow wheat noodles** are thick, spaghetti-like noodles made from wheat flour and egg. Substitute fresh spaghetti or fettucini if you cannot find them. **Dried rice vermicelli** has very fine rice threads that must be plunged into hot water to soften before use. **Rice stick noodles** (also known as "river noodles", *kway teow* or *hofun*) are wide, flat rice noodles sold fresh in Asian markets. If not available, use **dried rice stick noodles** instead.

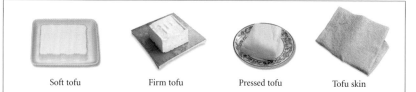

| Soft tofu | Firm tofu | Pressed tofu | Tofu skin |

Tofu or bean curd comes in various forms. **Soft tofu** is silky and smooth but difficult to cook because it falls apart. **Firm tofu** holds its shape well when cut or cooked and has a strong, slightly sour taste. **Pressed tofu** is firm tofu that has been compressed to expel most of the moisture. **Tofu skin** is the dried skin that forms on top of boiling soy milk; it is dried and sold in sheets as a wrapper, or as *tau fu kee*, a dried twisted tofu skin added to meat or vegetable dishes.

Oyster sauce is a soy-based sauce with oyster extract. Vegetarians should look for a version sold as "mushroom oyster sauce"

Palm sugar is made from the distilled juice of various palm fruits and varies in color from golden to dark brown. It has a rich flavor similar to dark brown

sugar or maple syrup, which makes a good substitute.

Rice wine is frequently used in Chinese cooking. Japanese sake, *mirin* or a dry sherry may be used as substitutes.

Sesame Oil is extracted from sesame seeds that have been toasted, producing a dark, dense and highly aromatic oil that can be used for marinades, sauces and soups, or as a table condiment. Its nutty, smokey flavor has become a hallmark of north Asian cuisine.

Shallots are small, round onions with thin red skins that add a sweet oniony flavor to countless dishes. They are added to spice pastes or sliced, deep-fried and used as garnish.

Sichuan peppercorns, also known as Chinese pepper or flower pepper (*hua jiao*), have a sharp pun-

| Regular soy sauce | Dark soy sauce | Sweet soy sauce |

Soy sauce is a fermented sauce brewed from soybeans, water, wheat and salt. **Regular** or **light soy sauce** is very salty and used as a table dip and cooking seasoning. **Dark soy sauce** is denser and less salty and adds a smoky flavor to dishes. **Sweet soy sauce** is a thick, fragrant sauce used in marinades and sauces.

gency that tingles and slightly numbs the lips and tongue, an effect known in Chinese as *ma la* "numb hot". To obtain **ground Sichuan pepper**, simply dry-roast Sichuan peppercorns in a dry pan, then grind to a fine powder.

Tamarind is the fruit of the tamarind tree seed pot. The dried pulp is sold in packets or jars and generally still has some seeds and pod fibers mixed in. It is used as a souring agent in many dishes. To obtain **tamarind juice**, soak the pulp in warm water for 5 minutes, mash well and then strain and discard the seeds and fibers.

Wood ear mushrooms have very little flavor and are added to dishes for their crunchy texture and as a meat substitute. They are sold dried in plastic packets in most Asian supermarkets and comes in small, crinkly sheets. Soak them in water before using. Wash well and discard any hard bits in the center of the larger pieces.

Sambal Belachan (Shrimp Paste Chili Sauce)

3 red finger-length chilies, deseeded
1 tablespoon dried shrimp paste (*belachan*), roasted
1 teaspoon sugar
$1/_4$ teaspoon salt
1 tablespoon lime juice

Grind the chilies and *belachan* in a mortar. Then add the sugar, salt and lime juice, and mix well. Serve in small bowls with Black Sauce Hokkien Noodles (page 54).

Thai Red Curry Paste

1 tablespoon coriander seeds
1 teaspoon cumin seeds
5 dried red chilies, deseeded and soaked in hot water for 15 minutes
3 tablespoons sliced shallots
8 cloves garlic, smashed
2-3 thin slices galangal
2 tablespoons sliced lemongrass (tender inner part of bottom third only)
2 teaspoons grated kaffir lime rind
1 tablespoon chopped coriander roots
10 black peppercorns
1 teaspoon dried shrimp paste (*belachan*), roasted

Dry-fry the coriander and cumin seeds in a wok or frying pan over low heat for about 5 minutes, then grind to a powder in a blender. Add the remaining ingredients, except the shrimp paste, and grind well. Add the shrimp paste and grind again to obtain about $3/_4$ cup (180 ml) of fine-textured curry paste.

Wok-fried Carrots with Mushrooms

Black Chinese mushrooms have been a mainstay of Chinese cuisine for many centuries. Research has proven what Chinese cooks and herbalists have known since ancient times—that mushrooms give a powerful boost to the human immune system. The carrot, when combined with mushrooms, provides a crunchy counterpoint to the chewy texture of the mushrooms and contributes its own considerable nutritional value to this dish. For some extra color and variety, try adding half a cup of fresh or frozen green peas along with the carrots.

10–12 dried black
  Chinese mushrooms
2 carrots, washed, grated
  or thinly shredded
2 tablespoons oil
1 in (2¹/₂ cm) fresh
  ginger, thinly shredded
4 to 5 cloves garlic,
  minced
2 green onions (scallions),
  minced

Sauce
2 tablespoons rice wine
2 tablespoons soy sauce
1 teaspoon sesame oil
1 teaspoon sugar
¹/₂ teaspoon salt

1 Soak the dried mushrooms in hot water for 15 minutes, then drain, reserving the liquid. Remove the stems, then slice the caps very thinly.

2 Mix together all the Sauce ingredients in a small bowl and set aside.

3 Heat the oil in a wok over medium heat, then add the mushrooms, ginger, and garlic together. Stir-fry for 2 minutes, then add the sauce and continue to stir-fry for 1 minute more.

4 Add the carrots and ¹/₃ cup (80 ml) of the mushroom water. Stir to blend, cover wok with lid, reduce the heat to low, and cook for 3 to 4 minutes. Remove from the heat, stir in the green onions, transfer to a platter and serve.

Serves 4
Preparation time: **20 mins**
Cooking time: **10 mins**

Spinach with Garlic

12 oz (350 g) fresh
spinach or Chinese
peashoots (*dou miao*),
washed and stems
removed,
2 tablespoons oil
$1/2$ teaspoon salt
3 to 5 cloves garlic,
peeled and sliced

1 Wash and rinse the spinach well, then place in a colander to drain.
2 Heat the oil in a wok over high heat and add the salt.
3 Add the sliced garlic and the spinach, and turn carefully with a spatula to coat all the leaves with oil. Stir-fry for about 1 minute, or until all the leaves are wilted and have turned dark green. Transfer immediately to a serving dish.

Serves 4
Preparation time: 10 mins
Cooking time: 2 mins

Chinese peashoots (*dou miao*) are the delicate leaves at the top of pea plants. They are particularly good when stir-fried simply with a little oil and garlic. Substitute spinach or any other leafy green.

Broccoli with Ginger

1 1/2 lbs (700 g) fresh
broccoli
3 tablespoons oil
6 slices fresh ginger, finely
shredded
1 onion, cut into
crescents
1 tablespoon rice wine
mixed with 1 teaspoon
water
1/2 teaspoon salt

Serves 4
Preparation time: 15 mins
Cooking time: 5 mins

1 Cut the broccoli florets from the main stem, so that each floret retains its own stalk. Peel the tough skin from the stalks below the florets with a sharp paring knife. Cut the stalks into bite-sized pieces.
2 Heat the oil in a wok over medium heat and when hot, stir in the broccoli and ginger and stir-fry for about 1 minute, or until all the broccoli has turned darker green. Add the onions and cook for 1 more minute.
3 Add the rice wine and water and cover tightly with a lid, steaming the broccoli for 1 to 2 minutes.
4 Remove the lid, add the salt, and stir to blend, then transfer to a serving dish.

Snow Peas with Mushrooms

Snow peas are one of the favorite vegetables of Chinese cooks. Snow peas and mushrooms are a classic combination in Chinese cuisine because they harmonize the *yin* and *yang* qualities. This dish may be prepared with either fresh or dried mushrooms. If you like it hot, add a few fresh or dried chilies (cut lengthwise with seeds and fibers removed) to the oil before cooking the mushrooms, and let them scorch before adding the mushrooms. You may also prepare this dish exactly the same way with broccoli instead of snow peas but make sure that you peel the broccoli stalks first. Another variation in flavor is to add a whole star anise along with the mushrooms and ginger.

8 oz (250 g) fresh snow peas
20 dried black Chinese mushrooms
3 tablespoons oil
1 in (2$^1/_2$ cm) fresh ginger, minced
2 green onions (scallions), cut into sections

Sauce
1$^1/_2$ tablespoons soy sauce
1$^1/_2$ tablespoons rice wine
1 teaspoon sugar
$^1/_2$ teaspoon salt
1 teaspoon sesame oil

Serves 4
Preparation time: **20 mins**
Cooking time: **5 mins**

1 Wash the snow peas, snap off the tips, and pull off the strings.

2 Wipe the mushrooms with a damp cloth to remove any grit, cut away the stems, and cut in half, if large. If using dried black Chinese mushrooms, soak in hot water for 15 minutes and drain; trim away the stems and cut each cap into four slices.

3 Combine all the Sauce ingredients in a small bowl and set aside.

4 Heat 2 tablespoons of oil in a wok over medium heat, add the snow peas, and stir-fry until they turn bright green, about 1 minute. Remove from the heat and set aside.

5 Heat the remaining oil in the wok and, when hot, add the mushrooms and ginger. Stir-fry for about 2 minutes, add the Sauce mixture, and cook for 1 minute more.

6 Add the snow peas and the green onions and stir-fry for 1 more minute. Transfer to a serving dish.

Sichuan Green Beans with Dried Shrimp

3 tablespoons dried
shrimp, soaked in warm
water for 10 mins
$1/_2$ cup (125 ml) plus
2 tablespoons oil
1 lb (500 g) fresh green
beans, strings removed
5 cloves garlic, minced
3 slices ginger, minced
3 green onions (scal-
lions), chopped
1 tablespoon vinegar

Sauce
2 tablespoons rice wine
1 tablespoon water
1 teaspoon salt
1 tablespoon sugar

Serves 4
Preparation time: **12 mins**
Cooking time: **10 mins**

1 Combine the Sauce ingredients in a small bowl.
2 Drain the dried shrimp and chop finely. Set aside.
3 Heat the $1/_2$ cup (125 ml) of oil in a wok until hot,
add the beans and fry until they begin to crinkle and
become soft without burning. Remove and drain,
discard the oil.
4 Heat the remaining 2 tablespoons of oil in the wok
until hot, add the garlic, ginger, spring onions and
shrimp and stir-fry for 30 seconds.
5 Add the beans and stir to coat them well in the oil,
then add the Sauce, and cook for about 3 minutes.
6 Turn off the heat, stir in the vinegar until blended,
then remove to a serving dish.

Dried shrimp are tiny, orange, saltwater shrimp that
have been dried in the sun. They come in different
sizes. Available in Asian markets, they should look
orangy-pink and plump; avoid any with a grayish
appearance or with an unpleasant smell. Dried shrimp
will keep for several months.

Peashoots with Garlic and Ginger

1 lb (500 g) fresh
Chinese peashoots
(*dou miao*—see note)
or spinach
2 tablespoons oil
3 cloves garlic, minced
2 slices fresh ginger, thinly sliced

Sauce
1 teaspoon salt
1 teaspoon sugar
$1/_2$ teaspoon ground
Sichuan pepper
2 teaspoons rice wine
2 teaspoons sesame oil

Serves 4
Preparation time: **5 mins**
Cooking time: **5 mins**

1 Wash the peashoots carefully, and drain well. Remove and discard any wilted or yellowing leaves and tough stalks. Set aside.

2 Combine the Sauce ingredients and set aside.

3 Heat the oil in a wok until hot, add the garlic and ginger and stir-fry quickly to release the aromas, about 30 seconds. Add the peashoots, turning several times to coat evenly with oil, and immediately add the Sauce and continue to stir-fry for about 3 minutes, or until the leaves turn a darker green. Remove to a platter and serve immediately.

Chinese peashoots (*dou miao*) are the delicate leaves at the top of pea plants. They are particularly good when stir-fried simply with a little oil and garlic. Substitute spinach or any other leafy green.

Hot and Spicy Sichuan Tofu

This dish is said to have been the speciality made by an old woman in a night market in Sichuan. Her dish was so renowned that people would travel from all over the province just to taste it. An equally tasty vegetarian version of this traditional recipe may be prepared with finely chopped black Chinese mushrooms.

1 cup (5 oz/150 g) lean ground pork or chicken
2 cakes soft tofu (10 oz/300 g each), drained
2 red finger-length chilies, deseeded and minced
6 cloves garlic, minced
6 slices fresh ginger, minced
3 tablespoons oil
1 tablespoon black bean paste (*tau cheo*)
1 teaspoon red chili oil or chili paste
3 to 4 green onions (scallions), chopped
1 teaspoon Sichuan Pepper-Salt Powder (see note)

Marinade
1 teaspoon cornstarch
$1/2$ teaspoon sugar
1 teaspoon soy sauce
1 tablespoon rice wine
1 teaspoon sesame oil
$1/2$ teaspoon ground Sichuan pepper

Sauce
1 cup (250 ml) water or chicken stock
1 tablespoon sugar
1 teaspoon salt
1 tablespoon soy sauce
1 teaspoon sesame oil

1 Combine the ground meat and the Marinade ingredients in a bowl and set aside. Combine the Sauce ingredients and set aside. Cube the tofu, and finely chop the chilies, garlic, and ginger.

2 Heat the oil in a wok over high heat and add the chilies, garlic, and ginger, then stir-fry for 1 minute. Add the ground meat and continue to stir-fry for 1 more minute. Add the bean paste, and chili oil or paste and cook for 1 minute more.

3 Add the Sauce, stir well to blend, and bring it to a boil. Add the tofu, stirring gently to coat with the Sauce. Cover, reduce the heat to medium, and cook for about 8 minutes, stirring occasionally to prevent sticking.

4 Uncover, stir gently to mix, and remove from the heat. Place in a serving bowl and sprinkle with chopped green onions and Sichuan Pepper-Salt Powder before serving.

For the vegetarian version, soak 6 to 8 **dried black Chinese mushrooms** in hot water for 20 minutes. Drain, cut away the tough stems, then cut the caps into small pieces. Set aside on a plate and add in place of meat. Some chefs also like to sprinkle freshly chopped coriander leaves over the dish as a garnish. You may control the heat of the chili flavor by adjusting the amount of red chili oil or paste, and by scraping the seeds and fibers from the fresh chilies for a milder pungency.

To make **Sichuan Pepper-Salt Powder**, dry-roast 2 tablespoons Sichuan peppercorns with $1/2$ teaspoon salt in a dry pan, then grind to a fine powder.

Serves 4
Preparation time: **10 mins** Cooking time: **10 mins**

Fried Eggplant with Sichuan Meat Sauce

This dish makes use of a particular style of Sichuan seasoning that provides a highly aromatic blend of all the basic flavors—sweet, sour, salty, pungent, and bitter—in a sauce that has the subtle fragrance of the freshest seafood. To make this dish properly, you should use the long purple Asian eggplant. The traditional method of preparation uses your choice of ground meat, but you may substitute chopped dried black Chinese mushrooms instead for a vegetarian version, or simply prepare it without meat or mushrooms.

$1/2$ cup (125 ml) plus 2 tablespoons oil

4 slender Asian eggplants, (about $1 1/3$ lbs/600 g), cut in half, then quartered lengthwise

6 cloves garlic, minced

8 slices fresh ginger, minced

$1/2$ cup (4 oz/100 g) ground pork, beef, or chicken

1 tablespoon black bean chili paste

6 green onions (scallions), minced

Sauce

2 teaspoons soy sauce

2 teaspoons rice wine

1 teaspoon sesame oil

1 teaspoon vinegar

1 tablespoon sugar, or more to taste

$1/2$ teaspoon freshly ground black pepper

1 teaspoon salt

2 tablespoons water

1 Combine the Sauce ingredients and set aside.

2 Heat the $1/2$ cup of oil in a wok over high heat until hot, and add the eggplants. Stir-fry, turning frequently, until they change color and soften. Remove the eggplants and set on a rack or colander to drain.

3 Heat the remaining 2 tablespoons of oil until hot. Add the garlic and ginger and stir-fry for 1 minute. Add the ground meat and continue to stir-fry for 2 more minutes. Add the black bean chili paste and stir-fry for 30 seconds. Add the Sauce mixture and stir to blend all ingredients.

4 Add the cooked eggplants and stir-fry until evenly coated. Cover with a lid, and simmer for 3 to 4 minutes, or until tender and fragrant. Remove to a serving dish and sprinkle with minced green onions.

To make the vegetarian version, simply substitute **dried black Chinese mushrooms** for the meat. Chopped fresh coriander leaves may be sprinkled on top as well, to accent the flavors.

Serves 4
Preparation time: **15 mins**
Cooking time: **10 mins**

Tofu and Green Beans with Peanuts and Chili

This is a very typical Chinese home-style dish, combining nourishing ingredients that are easily kept in stock in the kitchen and cooking them with a selection of stimulating seasonings that really help *xia fan* ("get the rice down"). For variety, add some diced carrots or green peas along with the green beans. If you have any leftovers, stir-fry it with leftover rice.

2 tablespoons oil
1 tablespoon sesame oil
1 cake (10 oz/300 g) pressed or firm tofu, cut into cubes
2 to 4 red finger-length chilies, deseeded and then sliced
10 oz (300 g) green beans, strings removed
6 to 8 cloves garlic, minced
1 in (2$^1/_2$ cm) fresh ginger, minced
1 cup (5 oz/150 g) roasted unsalted peanuts, skins removed
2 to 3 green onions (scallions), cut into sections

Sauce
1 tablespoon soy sauce
1 tablespoon rice wine
1 teaspoon sesame oil
1 teaspoon sugar
$^1/_2$ teaspoon salt

1 Mix the Sauce ingredients in a small bowl and set aside.

2 Heat both oils in a wok over medium heat and when hot, add the tofu and chili. Stir-fry for 1 minute, and add the green beans, garlic, and ginger, and stir-fry vigorously for 1 to 2 minutes more.

3 Add the peanuts and the Sauce mixture, and stir-fry for 2 minutes.

4 Stir in the green onions, then transfer to a serving dish.

Serves 4
Preparation time: 20 mins
Cooking time: 5 mins

Curried Carrots with Grated Coconut

1 lb (500 g) carrots,
  peeled and diced
2 tablespoons oil
1 teaspoon urad dal
  (see note)
1 teaspoon mustard
  seeds
1 teaspoon fennel seeds
2 dried red chilies,
  deseeded and cut into
  pieces
1 medium onion, thinly
  sliced
2 green finger-length-
  chilies, deseeded and
  cut into pieces
2 sprigs curry leaves
  (see note)
$1/_2$ teaspoon asafoetida
  powder (see note)
$1/_2$ teaspoon ground
  turmeric
1 teaspoon ground
  cumin
$1/_2$ teaspoon ground red
  pepper or cayenne pep-
  per (see note)
$1^1/_4$ teaspoons salt
1 teaspoon sugar
$1/_2$ cup (125 ml) water
$1/_2$ cup (2 oz/50 g) grated fresh coconut

Serves 4–6
Preparation time: 20 mins
Cooking time: 20 mins

1 Peel and dice the carrots.

2 Heat the oil and stir-fry the urad dal until it turns golden brown. Add the mustard and fennel seeds, dried chilies, then fry until the mustard seeds pop and the dried chilies brown. Add the onion, green chilies, curry leaves and asafoetida powder. Stir-fry until the onion turns golden brown, then add the diced carrot, ground spices, salt, sugar and water.

3 Cover and cook until the carrot is tender and the moisture has evaporated; stirring occasionally.

4 Add the grated coconut and mix well, stir-fry over high heat for about 2 minutes and serve.

Asafoetida is a strong-smelling brown resin. Known in India as *hing*, it adds an onion flavor to cooked food and is believed to aid digestion. Often used in lentil dishes, it is sold in a box or tin as a solid lump, or in the form of powder. Use very small amounts—a pinch is enough. Keep well sealed when not in use. If you cannot get it, omit from the recipe.

Ground red pepper is a pungent red powder made from ground dried chili peppers, also known as cayenne pepper. Substitute dried red chili flakes or chili paste.

Curry leaves come in sprigs of 8–15, dark green leaves and are used to flavor Indian curries. Fresh curry leaves should be used within a few days of purchase. Dried curry leaves keep well if stored in a dry place. There is no good substitute. Curry leaves are available in Indian food stores and from internet grocers.

Urad dal or **blackgram dal** is sold either with its black skin on or husked, when it is creamy white in color. Any other type of dried lentils may be used in this dish instead, or you may omit them.

Wok-fried Napa Cabbage with Tofu Skins

12 oz (350 g) Chinese or Napa cabbage
1 sheet dried tofu skin (about 2$\frac{1}{2}$ oz/80 g), soaked in water for 10 minutes, then drained
1 tablespoon sesame oil
2 tablespoons oil
4 slices fresh ginger, thinly sliced

Sauce
1 tablespoon soy sauce
1 teaspoon vinegar
1 teaspoon rice wine
1 teaspoon sugar
1 teaspoon salt

Serves 4
Preparation time: **15 mins**
Cooking time: **10 mins**

1 Slice the cabbage leaves to a similar size. Cut the tofu skin into small strips.
2 Combine all the Sauce ingredients and set aside.
3 Heat the oil in a wok until hot but not smoking.
4 Add the tofu skin and stir-fry for 1 minute. Add the cabbage and ginger, and continue to stir-fry until the cabbage is tender, about 3 to 4 minutes.
5 Add the Sauce mixture, reduce the heat to low, and cook for 1 to 2 minutes. Transfer to a serving dish.

For a touch of chili flavor that does not overpower the whole dish, cut 1 to 2 dried chilies lengthwise, scrape away the seeds and fibers and add them to the hot sesame oil before the tofu skin. A sprinkling of Sichuan Pepper-Salt Powder (page 27) over the finished dish, plus a handful of chopped green onions (scallions), will also spice it up nicely without smothering the subtle flavors of the main ingredients.

Chinese cabbage or Napa cabbage has tightly packed white stems and pale green leaves. It has a mild, delicate taste and should only be cooked for a few minutes to retain its color and crunchy texture. Chinese cabbage is a good source of calcium, potassium and iron, and is often eaten in soups. Available year round in supermarkets.

Wok-fried Chinese Greens with Lentils

$^1/_2$ cup (4 oz/100 g) channa dal or chick-peas, washed and drained (see note)

3 cloves garlic

1 teaspoon ground turmeric

$^1/_4$ teaspoon salt

4 cups (1 liter) water

2 tablespoons oil

1 teaspoon urad dal (see note)

1 teaspoon mustard seeds

1 teaspoon cumin seeds

2 dried red chilies, deseeded and cut into pieces

1 small onion, thinly sliced

1 red finger-length chili, deseeded and sliced

14 oz (400 g) *choy sum* or *chye sim* (Chinese Flowering Cabbage), washed and cut into pieces, including the stalks (see note)

1 teaspoon salt

4 tablespoons grated fresh coconut

1 Place the channa dal, garlic, turmeric powder, salt and water in a pan. Bring to a boil and simmer until the dal is cooked but remains firm, about 20 minutes. Drain the cooked dal, reserving 4 tablespoons of the liquid.

2 Heat the oil in a wok and stir-fry the urad dal, mustard and cumin seeds, and dried chilies until the urad dal becomes golden brown.

3 Add the cooked channa dal, *chye sim*, salt, reserved liquid and grated coconut. Stir-fry until the *chye sim* are cooked.

Choy sum or chye sim, also known as *Chinese flowering cabbage*, is a leafy green vegetable with crisp crunchy stems. Available in supermarkets in Asia, it is now increasingly available in Western countries too. Substitute any other leafy greens.

Channa dal or Bengal gram resembles a yellow split pea but is smaller. Urad dal or blackgram dal is sold either with its black skin on or husked, when it is creamy white in color. Chickpeas or garbanzo beans make good substitutes.

Serves 4–6
Preparation time: 15 mins
Cooking time: 15 mins

Stir-fried Mixed Vegetables

1 cup (5 oz/150 g) fresh or frozen peas
2 tablespoons oil
8 oz (250 g) fresh or frozen corn kernels (about 1$^1/_2$ cups)
2 carrots, diced
1 bell pepper, diced
1 onion, diced
5 oz (150 g) green beans, ends and strings removed, diced
1 in ($^1/_2$ cm) fresh ginger, minced
1 teaspoon Sichuan Pepper-Salt Powder (see note)

Sauce
1 tablespoon soy sauce
1 tablespoon water
1 teaspoon sugar
$^1/_2$ teaspoon salt
1 teaspoon sesame oil

1 Remove the green peas from their pods if using fresh peas, or defrost the peas if frozen.

2 Combine the Sauce ingredients in a small bowl and set aside.

3 Heat the oil in a wok and, when hot, stir-fry the corn, carrot, bell pepper, onion, green beans, and ginger for 2 minutes.

4 Add the peas, and continue to cook for another 1 or 2 minutes.

5 Add the Sauce, reduce the heat and cook slowly for 3 to 4 minutes, then add the Sichuan Pepper-Salt Powder and stir for 1 more minute to completely blend the flavors. Serve immediately.

To make **Sichuan Pepper-Salt Powder**, dry-roast 2 tablespoons Sichuan peppercorns with $^1/_2$ teaspoon salt in a dry pan, then grind to a fine powder.

Serves 4
Preparation time: **15 mins**
Cooking time: **10 mins**

Fried Eggplant with Tamarind Chili Sauce

4 slender Asian egg-
plants (about 1$\frac{1}{3}$
lbs/600 g), stems
removed (see note)
4 tablespoons oil

Chili Paste
8–10 dried chilies
2–4 red finger-length
chilies, deseeded
6 shallots, peeled
2 cloves garlic, peeled
3 tablespoons oil
1 tablespoon tamarind
pulp soaked in 2
tablespoons water,
mashed and strained to
obtain the juice
1 tablespoon sugar
1 teaspoon salt

Serves 4
Preparation time: **15 mins**
Cooking time: **25 mins**

1 To make the Chili Paste, cut the dried chilies into short lengths and soak in warm water for 10 to 15 minutes until softened. Then deseed and drain. Grind the drained chilies, fresh chilies, shallots and garlic in a mortar or blender until smooth, adding a little oil if necessary to keep the blades turning.

2 Heat the oil in a wok over low heat and stir-fry the ground paste until the oil separates from the mixture, about 5 minutes. Add the tamarind juice, sugar and salt, and stir-fry for about 1 minute. Remove from the heat and set aside.

3 Cut the ends from the eggplants, then halve each eggplant lengthwise. Heat 2 tablespoons of the oil in a wok or skillet over medium heat and cook half the eggplants until lightly browned on both sides, about 7 minutes. Remove from the oil and drain on paper towels. Heat the remaining oil and cook the rest of the eggplant halves.

4 Place the cooked eggplants on a serving dish. Spoon the chili sauce over them and serve immediately.

If **Asian eggplants** are not available, use regular Mediterranean eggplants cut into long narrow strips, and then cook as directed.

Stir-fried Spinach with Black Bean Sauce

2 tablespoons oil
3 cloves garlic, minced
1 tablespoon black bean paste (*tau cheo*)
1 lb (500 g) water spinach or regular spinach, tough stems discarded, carefully washed and snipped into sections (see note)
1 red finger-length chili, deseeded and sliced (optional)

1 Heat the oil in a wok over high heat until very hot, and stir-fry the garlic and black bean paste, about 30 seconds.
2 Add the water spinach and red chili, reduce the heat to medium, and stir-fry continuously for about 3 minutes, or until wilted and the bean paste is evenly distributed. Remove from the heat and serve.

Water spinach, also known as *water convolvulus* or morning glory, is a leafy green vegetable with crunchy, hollow stems. It is commonly used in Southeast Asian and Chinese cooking. It must be washed thoroughly to remove dirt and sand, and the thick, tough ends of stems removed. If unavailable, substitute normal spinach.

Serves 4
Preparation time: **8 mins**
Cooking time: **10 mins**

Simple Wok-fried Green Beans

2 tablespoons oil
1 onion, thinly sliced
2 cloves garlic, minced
1 lb (500 g) green beans, trimmed and cut into lengths
2 slices fresh ginger, cut into fine strips
1 red finger-length chili, deseeded and cut into thin strips (optional)
$1/4$ teaspoon salt
1 teaspoon soy sauce
1 tablespoon rice wine
7 oz (200 g) bean sprouts
2 teaspoons black Chinese vinegar (see note)
2 teaspoons sesame oil
Fresh coriander leaves (cilantro), to garnish
Freshly ground black pepper, to taste

1 Heat the oil in a wok until very hot and stir-fry the onion, garlic, beans, ginger, and chilies (if using) for 30 seconds. Add the salt, soy sauce, and wine and stir-fry for another 4 to 5 minutes.

2 Add the bean sprouts and stir-fry for 1 minute. Add the vinegar and cook for another 30 seconds. Add the sesame oil, stir to mix, remove from the heat, and transfer to a platter and garnish with the fresh coriander leaves. Sprinkle the pepper to taste.

Black Chinese vinegar is made from rice, wheat and millet or sorghum. The best black vinegars are well-aged and have a complex, smoky flavor similar to balsamic, which may be substituted. Chinese cooks add black vinegar sparingly to sauces, dips and when braising meats.

Serves 4
Preparation time: 20 mins
Cooking time: 15 mins

Potato Threads with Five Spice Powder

Like chilies and tomatoes, potatoes were introduced to China from the West, as reflected in the Chinese word, *yang yu*, which means "foreign taro." But like virtually all forms of food brought to China, the Chinese have applied their own culinary genius to the preparation of potatoes, which they neither deep-fry like the French, nor bake like the Americans. Instead of five spice powder, you could try dusting the finished dish with some Sichuan Pepper-Salt Powder.

4 to 5 medium potatoes
3 tablespoons oil
1 teaspoon sugar
1 teaspoon salt
$1/2$ teaspoon five spice
  powder
2 green onions (scallions),
  minced (optional)

Serves 4
Preparation time: 10 mins
Cooking time: 10 mins

1 Wash the potatoes well but do not peel them. Using a grater, shred the potatoes into a bowl of cool salted water to keep them from turning brown.
2 Just before cooking, strain the shredded potatoes, but do not rinse, and place in a colander to drain.
3 Heat the oil in a wok over medium heat until hot but not smoking.
4 Add the potatoes and stir-fry, then add the sugar, salt, and five spice powder. Continue to cook over medium for 8 to 10 minutes, or until firm and tender. Add enough water as needed during cooking to prevent the shredded potato from sticking to the pan.
5 Transfer to a serving plate and sprinkle evenly with the minced green onions.

To make **Sichuan Pepper-Salt Powder**, dry-roast 2 tablespoons Sichuan peppercorns with $1/2$ teaspoon salt in a dry pan, then grind to a fine powder.

Spinach with Mushrooms and Tofu Skins

2 sheets dried tofu skin, soaked in water for 20 minutes and drained
1 cup ($^1/_2$ oz/15 g) dried white fungus mushrooms (optional), soaked for 30 minutes; drained (see note)
2 tablespoons oil
2 cloves garlic, crushed
3 slices fresh ginger
1 red finger-length chili, halved lengthwise, deseeded, and sliced (optional)
1 onion, thinly sliced
1 carrot, peeled and coarsely grated
$^1/_2$ teaspoon salt
1 teaspoon sugar
2 tablespoons water
1 teaspoon black Chinese vinegar (see note)
8 oz (250 g) spinach, rinsed well, thick stems removed and sliced
1 teaspoon freshly ground black pepper
2 teaspoons sesame oil

1 Slice the soaked tofu skins into strips. Shred the soaked fungus, if using. Set aside.
2 Heat the oil in a wok over high heat until very hot, and stir-fry the garlic, ginger, chilies, and onion for 2 minutes. Add the tofu skin, fungus and carrot. Stir-fry for a further 1 to 2 minutes.
3 Stir in the salt, sugar, and 2 tablespoons of water. Cover with a lid, reduce the heat to low, and cook for 6 minutes.
4 Add the vinegar, stir to mix, and put in the spinach, black pepper, and sesame oil and stir-fry for another 3 minutes or until the spinach is wilted and the stalks are cooked through.

White fungus mushrooms is also known as *white woodears*, and has a crunchy texture and a slightly sweet flavor. It is sold dried and must be soaked in water before using.

Black Chinese vinegar is made from rice, wheat and millet or sorghum. The best black vinegars are well-aged and have a complex, smoky flavor similar to balsamic, which may be substituted. Chinese cooks add black vinegar sparingly to sauces, dips and when braising meats.

Serves 4
Preparation time: 20 mins + 30 mins soaking time
Cooking time: 15 mins

Sweet and Sour Eggplant

3 heaping tablespoons (70 g) tamarind pulp soaked in 1$^1/_2$ cups (375 ml) water, mashed and strained to obtain the juice
4 slender Asian eggplants, about 1$^1/_3$ lbs (600 g)
1 cup (250 ml) oil
5 whole cloves
5 cardamom pods
2 green finger-length chilies, slit lengthwise
2 teaspoons ground red pepper
$^1/_2$ teaspoon ground turmeric
$^1/_2$ teaspoon ground cumin
1 tablespoon ground fennel
1 teaspoon *garam masala* (see note)
4 tablespoons caster sugar
Salt to taste

1 Cut the eggplants into quarters lengthwise, then into 1$^1/_2$ in (4 cm) lengths.
2 Heat the oil in a wok and fry the eggplants until half cooked. Drain and set aside.
3 Discard all but 2 tablespoons of the oil and fry the cloves, cardamom pods and green chilies until aromatic.
4 Add in the ground spice powders, salt and sugar, tamarind juice as well as the fried eggplant. Cook until the gravy has thickened and the eggplant tender.

Garam masala is an Indian blend of ground spices, usually including cinnamon, cardamon, cloves, fennel and black pepper. Pre-blended **garam masala** can be bought from any store specializing in spices. Store in an airtight jar away from heat or sunlight.

Ground red pepper is a pungent red powder made from ground dried chili peppers, also known as cayenne pepper. Substitute dried red chili flakes or chili paste.

Serves 4
Preparation time: **15 mins**
Cooking time: **15 mins**

Stir-fried Tomatoes with Onion and Pine Nuts

$^1/_3$ cup (2 oz/50 g) pine nuts
2 tablespoons oil
1 large onion, diced
2 green onions (scallions), cut into lengths
3 large ripe tomatoes, cut into wedges
$^1/_4$ teaspoon salt
1 teaspoon sugar
1 teaspoon soy sauce
Fresh coriander leaves (cilantro), to garnish

1 Dry-roast the pine nuts in a dry skillet over medium-low heat, stirring constantly, until they turn golden brown, about 2 to 3 minutes. Remove from the skillet and set aside.
2 Heat the oil in a wok over high heat until hot, and stir-fry the onions and green onions to release the aromas, about 30 seconds.
3 Add the tomatoes, pine nuts, salt, sugar, and soy sauce, and stir-fry continuously for 1 to 2 minutes. Remove from the heat, garnish with the coriander leaves, and serve immediately.

Serves 4
Preparation time: 10 mins
Cooking time: 5 mins

Fried Rice Stick Noodles with Chicken

1 lb (500 g) Chinese broccoli or regular broccoli (see note)
5 tablespoons oil
12 oz (350 g) dried rice stick noodles (*kway teow* or *hofun*), soaked in water for 10 minutes and drained
1 tablespoon dark soy sauce
1 large egg, beaten
3 cloves garlic, chopped
8 oz (250 g) chicken or pork, thinly sliced, or shrimp, shelled and deveined
1 tablespoon yellow bean paste
1 to 2 tablespoons fish sauce
$1^1/_2$ cups (375 ml) chicken stock
1 tablespoon cornstarch mixed with 2 tablespoons water
$^1/_4$ teaspoon ground white pepper

1 Cut the broccoli into lengths. Peel the tough stems and cut to the same size as the leafy portions.
2 Heat 2 tablespoons of the oil in a wok over high heat. Add the noodles and soy sauce and stir-fry for about 30 seconds. Push the noodles to the sides of the pan and add the egg. Stir the egg and noodles together and transfer to a serving platter.
3 Add the remaining oil to the same pan and heat. Add the garlic and stir-fry until golden, then stir-fry the meat until it changes color. Stir in the bean sauce and the fish sauce.
4 Stir in the greens, chicken stock, and cornstarch mixture, and continue cooking and stirring until the sauce is transparent. Pour the mixture over the noodles and sprinkle with the ground white pepper.

Chinese broccoli, also known as *kailan* or Chinese kale, has long, narrow stems and leaves, and small edible flowers. The stems are the tastiest part while the leaves are slightly bitter and are often discarded. Chinese broccoli is available fresh in Asian markets. Substitute with broccoli stems or broccolini.

Serves 4
Preparation time: **15 mins**
Cooking time: **10 mins**

Wok-fried Rice Vermicelli

8 cups (2 liters) water
2 teaspoons salt
8 oz (250 g) dried rice vermicelli (*beehoon* or *mifen*)
2 eggs
Salt and freshly ground black pepper, to taste
4 tablespoons oil
2 cakes firm tofu (10 oz/300 g each)
1 cup (4 oz/120 g) chicken meat, cut into thin strips
5 oz (150 g) fresh shrimp, peeled and deveined
1 tablespoon sugar
10 oz (300 g) bean sprouts, tails removed
6 stalks garlic chives (*gu cai*), cut into lengths

Seasoning Paste
3 red finger-length chilies, deseeded
5 shallots, peeled
5 cloves garlic, peeled
1 tablespoon black bean paste (*tau cheo*)

Garnishes
3 tablespoons Crispy Fried Shallots (see note)
2 green onions (scallions), sliced
4 calamansi limes or 2 regular limes, halved, to serve

Serves 4
Preparation time: 30 mins
Cooking time: 30 mins

1 To make the Seasoning Paste, grind the chilies, shallots, garlic and black bean paste to a smooth paste in a mortar or blender, adding a little water if necessary to keep the blades turning. Set aside.

2 Bring the water and 1 teaspoon of the salt to a boil in a pan. Add the *beehoon* and cook until al dente, about 2 to 3 minutes. Drain and set aside to cool.

3 Beat the eggs with a pinch of salt and pepper. Heat 1 teaspoon of the oil in a skillet and add the eggs. Swirl the pan to allow the eggs to spread out and make a thin omelet. When the omelet is lightly browned, flip it over and cook on the other side. Fold the omelet and remove from the pan. Slice into thin strips and set aside.

4 Halve the tofu and pat dry with paper towels. Heat the remaining oil in a wok and gently stir-fry the tofu until lightly browned on both sides, about 4 minutes. Set aside to drain and cool, then slice into thin strips.

5 Heat the oil in the wok over medium heat and stir-fry the Seasoning Paste until the oil separates from the mixture, about 3 to 5 minutes. Add the chicken and stir-fry until cooked, about 3 minutes. Then add the shrimp, tofu, sugar and the remaining salt, and stir-fry for 3 minutes until the shrimp are cooked.

6 Add the noodles and stir-fry for 3 minutes until the paste has spread evenly. Add the bean sprouts and chives, and cook until the vegetables are wilted but still crunchy, about 2 minutes.

7 Transfer to a serving platter and garnish with the omelet strips, Crispy Fried Shallots, green onions and serve the lime wedges on the side.

Crispy Fried Shallots are readily available in packets or jars in most supermarkets and Asian food stores. To make them at home, thinly slice several cloves of shallots as desired and stir-fry in hot oil over low heat for 1-2 minutes, stirring constantly, until golden brown and crispy.

Malaysian Egg Noodles with Chili

5 tablespoons oil
2 cakes firm tofu (10 oz/300g each)
1 onion, thinly sliced
4 cloves garlic, sliced
3/4 cup (4 oz/100 g) chicken meat, cut into thin strips
4 oz (100 g) fresh shrimp, peeled and deveined
1 tomato, cut into wedges
4 1/2 cups (10 oz/300 g) sliced cabbage
3 cups (5 oz/150 g) *chye sim* or *bok choy*, cut into short lengths
500 g (1 lb) fresh yellow wheat noodles (*mee*) or fettucini
2 eggs
2–3 tablespoons Crispy Fried Shallots (page 46)
2 green onions (scallions), thinly sliced
4 calamansi limes or 2 regular limes, cut into wedges

Sauce
1 tablespoon soy sauce
1 tablespoon dark soy sauce
2 tablespoons tomato ketchup
1 teaspoon salt
2 teaspoons sugar

Chili Paste
6 dried chilies
5 shallots, peeled
5 cloves garlic, peeled
1 teaspoon dried shrimp paste (*belachan*)

1 To make the Sauce, combine all the ingredients in a bowl and set aside.

2 To make the Chili Paste, first cut the dried chilies into lengths, soak in hot water to soften, then deseed and drain. Grind the chilies, shallots, garlic and *belachan* to a smooth paste in a mortar or blender, adding a little water if necessary to keep the blades turning. Heat 2 tablespoons of the oil in a wok over medium heat and stir-fry the paste until the oil separates from the mixture, about 3 to 5 minutes. Transfer to a bowl and wipe the wok clean.

3 Halve the tofu and pat dry with paper towels. Heat the rest of the oil in a wok over medium heat and stir-fry the tofu until lightly browned, about 4 minutes. Drain on paper towels, and when cool enough to handle, cut into long strips.

4 Heat the oil in the wok and stir-fry the onion and garlic until fragrant, about 2 minutes. Add the chicken and stir-fry for 3 minutes, then add the shrimp, tomato, cabbage and *chye sim*. Increase the heat to high and stir-fry for 2 minutes. Add the Chili Paste and tofu, and cook for 2 minutes. Add the Sauce and noodles, and stir-fry over high heat for 3 to 4 minutes.

5 Make a well in the center of the wok and add 2 teaspoons of oil. Add the eggs, scramble and allow to brown slightly. Mix all the ingredients together and serve, garnished with the Crispy Fried Shallots and green onions, and serve the lime halves on the side.

Mee Goreng tastes better when cooked in small batches. With a more manageable quantity in the wok, stir-frying to the preferred degree of doneness is easier to achieve. It is suggested that the ingredients in this recipe be divided into two halves and the cooking done in 2 batches.

Serves 4
Preparation time: 20 mins
Cooking time: 20–30 mins

Shrimp Pad Thai Noodles

This dish may also be prepared with meat or mixed seafood instead of shrimp. Simply substitute 10 oz (300 g) mixed seafood, chicken, pork, or beef.

4 tablespoons oil
4 shallots, minced
12 to 16 fresh shrimp, peeled and deveined
4 eggs
8 oz (250 g) dried rice stick noodles (*kway teow* or *hofun*), soaked in warm water until soft and drained
1 teaspoon dried chili flakes or ground red pepper
4 cups (7 oz/200 g) bean sprouts
1 small bunch garlic chives (*gu cai*), cut into lengths
4 tablespoons ground roasted peanuts
2 limes, halved, to serve

Sauce
1 tablespoon tamarind pulp soaked in 2 tablespoons water, mashed and strained to obtain the juice
2 tablespoons shaved palm sugar or dark brown sugar
2 tablespoons fish sauce
$1/2$ teaspoon ground white pepper
Pinch of salt

1 Combine all the Sauce ingredients in a saucepan. Cook for 1 to 2 minutes over medium heat, stirring constantly, until the sugar is dissolved. Set aside.
2 Heat the oil in a wok over medium heat. Add the shallots and stir-fry for about 1 minute until fragrant. Add the shrimp and stir-fry until pink. Reduce the heat and add the eggs. Mix well and add the rice noodles. Increase the heat and stir-fry for about 1 minute. Add the Sauce ingredients and chili flakes. Mix well and stir-fry for 30 seconds to 1 minute. Add half the bean sprouts and chives and stir-fry for another 30 seconds before removing from the heat.
3 Serve hot on individual plates, garnished with the remaining fresh bean sprouts and chives, peanuts and limes.

Serves 4
Preparation time: **10 mins**   Cooking time: **10 mins**

Beef Rice Stick Noodles

4 tablespoons oil
3 cloves garlic, minced
5 oz (150 g) ground beef or thinly sliced beef
1 egg
1 cup (2$^1/_2$ oz/80 g) baby corn
1 cup (4 oz/100 g) cauliflower florets
1 cup (4 oz/100 g) asparagus, cut into lengths
1 cup (4 oz/100 g) Chinese broccoli (*kailan*)
 or regular broccoli, cut into lengths (see note)
8 oz (250 g) dried rice stick noodles (*kway teow* or
 hofun), soaked in warm water until soft and drained

Sauce
1 tablespoon fish sauce
1 tablespoon oyster sauce
1 teaspoon sugar
1 teaspoon dark soy sauce
$^1/_2$ teaspoon ground white pepper

1 Heat the oil in a wok over medium heat, add the garlic, and stir-fry. Add the beef and stir-fry until browned.
2 Add the egg and stir well. Add all the vegetables and the noodles and stir-fry for 3 to 4 minutes, or until the vegetables are cooked.
3 Stir in the fish sauce, oyster sauce, sugar, soy sauce, and ground white pepper. Stir well, and serve immediately.

Chinese broccoli, also known as *kailan* or Chinese kale, has long, narrow stems and leaves, and small edible flowers. The stems are the tastiest part while the leaves are slightly bitter and are often discarded. Chinese broccoli is available fresh in Asian markets. Substitute with broccoli stems or broccolini.

Serves 4
Preparation time: 1 hour
Cooking time: 10 mins

Black Sauce Chinese Noodles

1 lb (500 g) fresh or dried wheat noodles or fettucini
3 tablespoons oil
5 cloves garlic, sliced
1 1/4 cups (5 oz/150 g) thinly sliced chicken meat
5 oz (150 g) medium shrimp, peeled and deveined
5 oz (150 g) squid, cut into bite-sized pieces
3 cups (5 oz/150 g) sliced *bok choy* or *choy sum*
2 cups (4 oz/100 g) sliced round or Chinese cabbage
Shrimp Paste Chili Sauce (Sambal Belachan, page 7), to
  serve
2 limes, cut into wedges, to serve

Sauce
2 1/2 tablespoons dark soy sauce
1 tablespoon soy sauce
1 tablespoon oyster sauce
2 teaspoons sugar
1/2 teaspoon salt
1/4 teaspoon ground white pepper
2 teaspoons cornstarch
1 cup (250 ml) water

1 To make the Sauce, mix all the ingredients together
in a bowl and set aside.
2 Bring 6 cups (1 1/2 liters) of water to a boil in a pan.
Add the dried noodles, bring to a boil again and cook
for 3 to 4 minutes until the noodles are tender. If using
fresh noodles, blanch briefly to revive them. Then drain,
rinse in cold water and set aside to drain in a colander.
3 Heat the oil in a wok over high heat and stir-fry the
garlic until golden brown, about 1 minute. Add the
chicken and stir-fry for 2 minutes. Then add the
shrimp and squid, and cook for 1 to 2 minutes.
4 Add the Sauce and bring to a boil. Add the noodles
and stir-fry gently for 2 to 3 minutes. Add the vegetables and stir-fry for 2 to 3 minutes until slightly wilted
but still crunchy. Remove from the heat and serve with
a small bowl of Shrimp Paste Dip with lime halves on
the side.

Serves 4
Preparation time: 30 mins   Cooking time: 20 mins

Fried Bean Thread Noodles

4 tablespoons oil
3 cloves garlic, chopped
8 oz (250 g) thinly sliced pork, beef or chicken
3 tablespoons woodear mushrooms, soaked in hot
  water for 20 minutes, and stems removed
1 carrot, peeled and finely shredded
1 stalk celery, shredded
7 oz (200 g) dried bean thread noodles, soaked
  10 minutes, drained, and cut into lengths (see note)
$1/4$ cup (60 ml) chicken stock or cold water
2 large eggs, lightly beaten
1 tablespoon vinegar
3 tablespoons fish sauce
1 teaspoon sugar
$1/2$ teaspoon salt
$1/2$ teaspoon freshly ground black pepper
2 green onions (scallions), cut into lengths

1 Heat 3 tablespoons of the oil in a wok over medium-high heat. Stir-fry the garlic until light brown, 2 to 3 minutes. Add the meat, and stir-fry until the meat cooks through, 2 to 3 minutes.
2 Add the mushrooms, carrots, and celery. Stir until well mixed. Stir in the noodles, then the stock and mix well. Push the noodles up onto the sides of the pan.
3 Add the remaining oil. Pour in the eggs and scramble them, then mix with the contents of the pan. Stir in the vinegar, fish sauce, sugar, salt, pepper, and green onions. Remove to a serving platter.

Bean thread noodles, also known as "cellophane" or "glass" noodles, are thin, clear strands made from mung bean starch and water. Soak in hot water for 15 minutes to soften. Available from Asian food stores.

Serves 2
Preparation time: 10 mins
Cooking time: 15 mins

Classic Shrimp Fried Rice

The idea of stir-frying rice with other ingredients originated in China and has made its way throughout Asia. Generally, a serving of fried rice with all the trimmings makes a filling meal; this version is very light and delicate. Note that using leftover cooked rice works best for stir-frying because the grains are slightly dry and they separate easily.

3 tablespoons oil
2 cloves garlic, minced
8 oz (250 g) shrimp, peeled and deveined
1 small onion, cut into wedges
1 ripe tomato, cut into wedges
2 eggs, beaten
4 cups (14 oz/400 g) cooked rice
1 green onion (scallions), sliced
Sprigs of coriander leaves (cilantro), to garnish

Seasoning
1 tablespoon soy sauce
1 tablespoon fish sauce
$1/2$ teaspoon salt
$1/4$ teaspoon freshly ground white pepper

1 Combine the Seasoning ingredients in a small bowl and mix well. Set aside.

2 Heat the oil in a wok over high heat, turning to grease the sides. Stir-fry the minced garlic for about 30 seconds until fragrant and golden brown. Add the shrimp and stir-fry until pink and are just cooked, about 30 seconds, then add the onion and tomato and mix well. Push the ingredients to the sides of the wok and make a well in the center. Add the egg and allow the white to firm, then scramble. Add the rice, reduce the heat to medium and stir-fry for 3 to 5 minutes, constantly mixing and tossing until the rice grains are separated and the rice is heated through. Add the Seasoning and stir-fry for a further 1 to 2 minutes until all the ingredients are well blended. Stir in the green onion, mix well and remove from the heat.

3 Transfer the fried rice to individual serving bowls. Garnish with sprigs of coriander leaves (cilantro) and serve hot.

Serves 2–3
Preparation time: **10 mins**
Cooking time: **8 mins**

Homestyle Chinese Fried Rice

Fried rice is probably the single most commonly prepared dish in kitchens of Asian homes, and it is rarely prepared from scratch. Instead, it utilizes leftover rice along with leftover vegetables, tofu, meat scraps, and other items to prepare a tasty hot meal that is quick and easy to cook, requiring no shopping. You may allow your culinary creativity to express itself freely when cooking fried rice at home, while also applying the "waste not, want not" philosophy of the Asian kitchen.

Assorted leftover ham, chicken, bacon, tofu and vegetables (except leafy greens), such as carrots, corn, mushrooms, peas, green beans, and onion

$1/4$ cup (60 ml) oil

3 to 4 cloves garlic, minced

1 bell pepper, deseeded and thinly sliced

1 large egg, lightly beaten

4 cups (14 oz/400 g) cooked rice, white or brown (see note)

2 to 3 green onions (scallions), minced

1 teaspoon salt

1 teaspoon freshly ground black pepper

Serves 4
Preparation time: 15 mins
Cooking time: 10 mins

1 Dice all the meat and vegetable leftovers into small pieces, then set aside in a bowl.

2 Heat the oil in a wok over high heat. When hot, add the garlic, chili, and leftovers and stir-fry quickly for about 1 minute.

3 Add the egg, stirring quickly to scramble. Add the cooked rice and continue to stir-fry until the rice and vegetables are well mixed, when the rice begins to brown, about 3 to 5 minutes.

4 Sprinkle on the green onions, salt, and pepper, and continue to stir and turn for another 1 to 2 minutes. Transfer to a serving dish, or to individual rice bowls.

Brown rice is rice with its golden-brown bran intact. It has a nutty texture and more fiber than milled white rice, and requires more water as well as longer cooking time.

The cooked rice should be dry and firm when preparing this dish; soggy rice does not work well in this recipe. If you have leftover meat such as stir-fried fish, they may be added along with the vegetables and tofu. A sprinkling of minced fresh coriander leaves and a dusting of Sichuan Pepper-Salt Powder (page 27) on top of the finished dish provide some stimulating flavors that will add a lot of character.

Vegetarian Fried Brown Rice

This is a good way to use leftover rice, particularly brown rice, which does not get as soggy as white rice. You may use almost any combination of vegetables—such as turnip, bell peppers, cooked corn, fresh mushrooms, chopped cabbage, diced squash—to prepare this dish, and it may stand alone as a meal. This is a typical example of the pragmatic spirit of Asian homestyle cooking, which always regards leftovers as the foundation of another good meal.

10 dried black Chinese mushrooms
3 tablespoons oil
1 onion, sliced into crescents
3 to 4 cloves garlic, minced
3 to 4 slices fresh ginger, minced
2 carrots, diced
12 broccoli florets, stems peeled and diced
1 green bell pepper, diced
1 cup (5 oz/150 g) fresh or frozen peas
3 cups (10 oz/300 g) cooked rice, white or brown (see note)

Sauce
1 tablespoon soy sauce
1 teaspoon rice wine
$^1/_2$ teaspoon sugar
1 teaspoon salt
1 teaspoon sesame oil

1 Soak the dried black Chinese mushrooms for 15 minutes in hot water, drain and reserve $^1/_2$ cup (125 ml) of the liquid. Remove the stems. Squeeze the excess moisture from the mushrooms and slice each cap into 4 to 6 strips.

2 Combine all the Sauce ingredients in a bowl and set aside.

3 Heat the oil in a wok over high heat and stir-fry the mushrooms, onions, garlic, and ginger for 1 minute. Add the Sauce mixture, then add the carrots, broccoli, bell pepper, and peas. Stir-fry for 3 minutes.

4 Add the cooked rice and continue to stir until all the ingredients are well mixed, then add the mushroom water and mix through until well combined.

5 Reduce the heat, cover with the lid, and cook for 3 to 4 minutes, then transfer to serving platter.

Brown rice is rice with its golden-brown bran intact. It has a nutty texture and more fiber than milled white rice, and requires more water as well as longer cooking time.

Serves 4
Preparation time: **20 mins**
Cooking time: **15 mins**

Pineapple Fried Rice

8 oz (250 g) fresh squid (6 to 7 small squid)
4 cups (14 oz/400 g) cooked rice
1 large fresh pineapple
4 tablespoons oil
2 cloves garlic, minced
2 medium onions, chopped
1 tablespoon curry powder
8 fresh shrimp (about 5 oz/150 g), peeled and deveined
5 oz (150 g) fresh or canned crab meat (about 1 cup)
1 green or red bell pepper, diced
1 tomato, diced
4 tablespoons yellow raisins
1 teaspoon sugar
2 tablespoons soy sauce
$3/_4$ teaspoon ground white pepper

1 Rinse each squid thoroughly, detaching and discarding the head. Remove the cartilage in the center of the tentacles. Remove the reddish-brown skin from the body sac and scrape the inside of the body sac with the dull edge of a knife. Rinse well and slice into thin strips.
2 Place the rice in a large bowl and toss it gently to separate the grains. Set aside.
3 With the sharp point of a knife, mark a rectangular outline on the pineapple and cut along these lines. Remove the rectangular section and hollow out the fruit in the center, creating a bowl but not cutting through. Dice the pineapple to yield about $3/_4$ cup ($4^1/_2$ oz/125 g) of the fruit. Set aside.
4 Heat the oil in a wok over medium heat, turning to grease the sides. Add the garlic and stir-fry until fragrant, about 1 minute, then add the onions and curry powder. When fragrant, add the seafood and stir-fry until the shrimp turn pink and are just cooked.
5 Add the rice, diced pineapple, bell pepper, tomato and raisins. Mix well and stir-fry for about 3 minutes. Season with the sugar, soy sauce and pepper. Stir-fry for another minute until well mixed before removing from heat.
6 Serve the fried rice in the pineapple as shown.

Serves 4
Preparation time: 30 mins   Cooking time: 15 mins

Indian Fried Rice

3 tablespoons oil
1 tablespoon fresh
  ginger, minced
1 cup (5 oz/150 g)
  onion, diced
1 tablespoon curry
  powder
8 oz (250 g) chicken or
  lamb, sliced into thin
  strips
2 cups (14 oz/400 g)
  fresh tomatoes, diced
1 cup (5 oz/150 g) fresh
  or frozen peas
Salt and freshly ground
  white pepper to taste
4 cups (14 oz/400 g)
  freshly cooked rice,
  cooled
2 tablespoons mint
  leaves or parsley,
  chopped

1 Heat the oil in a wok over medium heat and stir-fry the ginger and onion until fragrant. Add the curry powder and stir-fry for about 2 minutes until aromatic.
2 Add the chicken or lamb strips and stir-fry over high heat for 2 minutes.
3 Add the tomatoes, peas, salt, pepper, and rice and stir-fry for about 5 minutes. Garnish with mint leaves or parsley and serve.

Leftover roast meat can be used as a substitute for fresh meat. If fresh diced tomatoes are unavailable, you can use 2 tablespoons tomato purée or ketchup. Cooked rice should be fluffy; overnight or leftover rice is ideal.

Serves 4
Preparation time: **15 mins**
Cooking time: **10 mins**

Thai Fried Rice

Tightly covered and refrigerated, the Chili Dipping Sauce will keep for up to 2 weeks. It can be spooned over just about any dish: soups, salads, grilled meats, fish, noodles, and curries. Use a dry spoon.

4 cups (14 oz/400 g) cooked rice
4 tablespoons oil
5 cloves garlic, minced
8 oz (250 g) chicken, pork or beef, thinly sliced
2 eggs
4 tablespoons soy sauce
1 teaspoon sugar
$1/2$ teaspoon ground white pepper
2 green onions (scallions), thinly sliced
1 cucumber, peeled and sliced, to serve
2 tomatoes, cut into wedges, to serve
1 lime, halved, to serve

Chili Dipping Sauce
4 tablespoons freshly squeezed lime juice
3 tablespoons fish sauce
2 bird's-eye chilies, thinly sliced
2 cloves garlic, minced

1 Make the Chili Dipping Sauce first by combining all the ingredients in a bowl, stirring to mix well. This makes about $3/4$ cup (175 ml) of sauce. Transfer to a serving bowl and set aside.

2 Place the rice in a large bowl and toss it gently to separate the grains. Set aside.

3 Heat the oil in a wok over high heat, turning to grease the sides. Add the garlic and stir-fry for about 1 minute until fragrant. Add the meat and stir-fry for 1 to 2 minutes until the meat changes color, then add the eggs and mix well. Add the rice and stir-fry for several minutes, mixing and tossing constantly until the rice is heated through. Finally add the soy sauce, sugar and pepper. Stir-fry for a further 1 to 2 minutes and remove from heat.

4 Arrange the rice on a serving platter and scatter the thinly sliced green onions on top. Serve immediately with the cucumber, tomatoes, lime and Chili Dipping Sauce.

This dish always works better with cooked rice prepared a day or two in advance. So consider making extra rice whenever you cook for another meal.

Serves 4
Preparation time: 20 mins
Cooking time: 12 mins

Vietnamese Garlic Shrimp

1 1/2 lbs (700 g) fresh shrimp, peeled and deveined
3 tablespoons oil
4 cloves garlic, minced
1 to 2 red finger-length chilies, deseeded and minced
1 tablespoon oyster sauce
Sprigs of coriander leaves (cilantro), to garnish

Marinade
2 teaspoons minced garlic
1 tablespoon fish sauce
1/4 teaspoon salt

1 Combine the Marinade ingredients in a large bowl and mix well. Place the shrimp in the Marinade and mix until well coated. Allow to marinate for at least 30 minutes.
2 Heat the oil in a wok or large skillet over high heat, add the shrimp and stir-fry until cooked, 2 to 3 minutes. Remove from the heat and transfer to a serving platter.
3 Reheat the remaining oil in the skillet over medium heat. Stir-fry the garlic and chilies for 1 to 2 minutes, until fragrant, and season with the oyster sauce. Remove from the skillet and spoon the mixture over the shrimp. Garnish with coriander leaves (cilantro) and serve hot with steamed rice.

Serves 4
Preparation time: 10 mins + 30 mins to marinate
Cooking time: 7 mins

Pepper Crabs with Garlic

2 to 3 fresh medium crabs (3 lbs/1$^1/_2$ kgs)
3 tablespoons oil
1 tablespoon minced garlic
1 tablespoon freshly ground black pepper
$^1/_2$ teaspoon sugar
$^1/_2$ teaspoon salt
$^1/_2$ cup (125 ml) chicken stock
1 green onion (scallions), thinly sliced

Serves 4
Preparation time: 20 mins
Cooking time: 15 mins

1 Scrub and rinse the crabs thoroughly. Detach the claws from each crab. Lift off the carapace and discard. Scrape out any roe and discard the gills. Rinse well, halve the crabs with a cleaver and crack the claws with a mallet.
2 Heat the oil in a wok over high heat and stir-fry the garlic and black pepper until fragrant, about 30 seconds. Add the crabs and stir-fry for 2 to 3 minutes, seasoning with the sugar and salt. Add the chicken stock, mix well and simmer for 3 to 5 minutes, covering the wok. Finally add the green onion, stir well and remove from the heat.
3 Transfer the crabs to a serving platter and serve immediately.

Sweet Chili Sauce Shrimp

Shrimp is one of the most popular seafoods throughout the world, but no one cooks them better than Chinese chefs. In this Sichuan version, they are marinated in ginger and wine, then cooked very quickly with garlic, green onions (scallions), and a savory chili sauce. For best results, use fresh shrimp but frozen shrimp may also be used as long as they are top quality and fresh frozen.

1 lb (500 g) fresh or frozen raw shrimp, shelled and deveined
2 tablespoons oil
3 to 4 cloves garlic, minced
4 green onions (scallions), cut into lengths

Marinade
2 tablespoons rice wine
1 teaspoon sesame oil
1 tablespoon ginger, minced
$1/2$ teaspoon sugar

Sauce
2 tablespoons bottled chili sauce
1 teaspoon tomato ketchup
$1/2$ teaspoon sugar
1 teaspoon salt
1 teaspoon sesame oil
2 teaspoons cornstarch dissolved in $1/2$ cup (125 ml) water

1 Place the shrimp in a bowl. Combine the Marinade ingredients, stir, then pour over the shrimp, mixing well with a spoon or using your fingers. Set aside to marinate for 15 to 20 minutes.
2 Combine the Sauce ingredients and set aside.
3 Heat the oil in a wok until hot. Add the garlic and the marinated shrimp and stir-fry swiftly until the shrimp turn pink and the flesh becomes firm, about 1 to 2 minutes. Add the sauce and stir-fry for a further 1 minute to mix the ingredients.
4 Add the green onions and cook for 30 seconds more, then remove to a platter, and serve immediately.

Serves 4
Preparation time: 30 mins
Cooking time: 5 mins

Delicious Sliced Fish with Black Bean Sauce

You may use any type of firm-fleshed fish for this recipe—such as tuna, halibut, snapper, sea bass, or swordfish. Different types of fish cook at slightly different rates, and the size of the pieces also influence the cooking time—so be careful not to overcook, as that will make the fish tough. This dish may be garnished with minced fresh coriander leaves (cilantro).

$1^1/_2$ lbs (700 g) fish steaks or fillets
3 tablespoons oil
3–4 cloves garlic, minced
$1^1/_2$ to 2 tablespoons black bean paste (*tau cheo*)
6 green onions (scallions), cut into sections
1 teaspoon sugar
1 teaspoon coarsely ground black pepper
2 sprigs fresh coriander leaves (cilantro), minced, as garnish (optional)

Marinade
2 tablespoons rice wine
1 teaspoon sesame oil
3 tablespoons fresh ginger, minced

1 Cut the fish into bite-sized chunks. If using steaks, remove the bones. Place the fish in a mixing bowl.
2 Mix the Marinade ingredients, pour over the fish, and turn to coat the fish evenly. Cover and set aside to marinate for about 30 minutes.
3 Heat the oil in a wok over high heat, and add the marinated fish and garlic. Stir-fry for 1 to 2 minutes, until the fish changes color. Add the black bean paste and continue to cook for another 1 to 2 minutes.
4 Add the green onions, sugar, and coarsely ground black pepper, stirring for 1 more minute to blend the flavors. Transfer to a serving dish.

Serves 4
Preparation time: 30 mins
Cooking time: 5 mins

Tangy Tamarind Shrimp

15–20 dried chilies, deseeded and cut into short
  lengths
$1/_2$ teaspoon dried shrimp paste (*belachan*)
10 shallots, peeled
4 tablespoons oil
1 tablespoon tamarind pulp soaked in 3 tablespoons
  water, mashed and strained to obtain the juice
$1–1^1/_4$ lbs (500–600 g) fresh shrimp, peeled and
  deveined
3 kaffir lime leaves, torn (optional, see note)
1 medium onion, cut into 10 wedges
2 teaspoons sugar
1 teaspoon salt

1 Soak the chilies in warm water for 10 to 15 minutes
to soften. Then deseed and drain. Grind the chilies,
belachan and shallots in a mortar or blender to a
paste, adding a little oil if necessary to keep the blades
turning.
2 Heat the oil in a wok over low heat and gently stir-
fry the ground ingredients for 6 to 8 minutes until
the oil surfaces.
3 Add the tamarind juice and cook, stirring frequently, for 6 to 8 minutes until most of the moisture has
evaporated. Add the shrimp, kaffir lime leaves and
onion, and stir-fry over low to medium heat for 10
minutes. Add the sugar and salt, and stir-fry until dissolved. Serve hot.

Kaffir lime leaves are the fragrant leaves of the kaffir
lime plant. The leaves are used whole in soups and
curries, or shredded finely and added to salads.

Serves 4
Preparation time: **30 mins**
Cooking time: **30 mins**

Vietnamese Caramel Fish

The Vietnamese typically use catfish for this dish, but any firm-fleshed fish will do. Use whole fish or large slices of cross-cut fillets as these keep whole better. The fish is delicious served with steamed rice.

2 tablespoons oil
$1^1/_2$ lbs (700 g) catfish fillets, cut into thick slices
$^1/_2$ in (1 cm) fresh ginger root, peeled and grated
Sprigs of coriander leaves (cilantro), to garnish

Caramel Sauce
$^2/_3$ cup (4 oz/135 g) sugar
$^1/_2$ cup (125 ml) fish sauce
8 shallots, thinly sliced
$^1/_2$ teaspoon freshly ground black pepper

1 To prepare the Caramel Sauce, heat the sugar over low heat in a skillet, stirring constantly, until it begins to melt and caramelize, 3 to 5 minutes. Remove from the heat and add the fish sauce. Return the skillet to the heat and bring the mixture to a boil over medium heat. Simmer uncovered for 3 to 5 minutes, stirring constantly until the mixture turns into a thick syrup. Add the shallot and black pepper, mix well and remove from the heat.
2 Heat the oil in a wok or skillet over medium heat. Add the fish and stir-fry for 2 to 3 minutes. Add the ginger and Caramel Sauce, and bring the mixture to a boil. Reduce the heat to low and simmer uncovered for 5 more minutes, until the fish is cooked. Remove from the heat and transfer to a serving platter.
3 Garnish with sprigs of coriander leaves (cilantro) and serve hot with steamed rice.

Serves 4–6
Preparation time: **10 mins**
Cooking time: **25 mins**

Simple Curried Fish Steaks

1 lb (500 g) fish fillets or steaks
4 tablespoons oil
$^1/_2$ teaspoon cumin seeds
$^1/_4$ teaspoon fenugreek
$^1/_4$ teaspoon fennel seeds
$^1/_4$ teaspoon mustard seeds
3 tablespoons minced ginger
3 tablespoons minced garlic
3 tablespoons minced green chili
1 teaspoon ground turmeric
3 tablespoons mustard seeds, ground
Scant 1 cup (200 ml) water
1 teaspoon salt

1 Heat half the oil and fry the fish slices for 3 minutes on both sides. Drain and set aside with the oil and the juice.
2 In a large saucepan or wok, heat the remaining oil and fry the cumin, fenugreek, fennel and mustard seeds until aromatic. Add in the rest of the ingredients except for the fried fish slices and cook for 5 minutes, stirring often.
3 When the gravy bubbles, gently lower the fish slices into the pan and simmer for 3 minutes. Remove and serve.

Serves 4
Preparation time: 10 mins
Cooking time: 25 mins

Sliced Fish with Mushrooms and Ginger

The perfect duo, fresh ginger and bean sauce, perk up this stir-fried fish. For the snappiest flavor, look for fresh young ginger.

3 tablespoons oil
3 cloves garlic, minced
3 in (8 cm) fresh ginger root, peeled and cut into thin strips
3 fresh black Chinese mushrooms, stems discarded, caps sliced into thin strips
1 tablespoon *hoisin* sauce (see note)
$^1/_4$ cup (60 ml) chicken stock
1 lb (500 g) flounder or other white fish fillets, thinly sliced
2 teaspoons fish sauce
1 teaspoon sugar
$^1/_2$ teaspoon freshly ground black pepper
1 to 2 red finger-length chilies, deseeded and cut into thin strips (optional)
1 green onion (scallions), cut into lengths, to garnish
Sprigs of coriander leaves (cilantro), to garnish

1 Heat the oil in a wok or skillet over medium heat. Stir-fry the garlic, ginger and mushrooms for 2 to 3 minutes, until fragrant. Add the *hoisin* sauce and stir-fry for a few seconds, then add the chicken stock and bring the mixture to a boil. Stir in the fish pieces and simmer uncovered, seasoning with the fish sauce, sugar and black pepper, until cooked, 3 to 5 minutes. Finally add the chili (if using), mix well and remove from the heat.

2 Transfer to a serving platter, garnish with the green onion and coriander leaves (cilantro), and serve hot with steamed rice.

Hoisin sauce consists of fermented soybeans, garlic, chilies, and vinegar. The sauce is thick and dark and has a sweet, salty flavor. Commercially bottled or canned hoisin sauce is available in most grocery sauce.

Serves 4
Preparation time: 8 mins
Cooking time: 10 mins

Quick Curried Shrimp

1 lb (500 g) shrimp, shelled

3 tablespoons oil

3 medium onions, finely chopped

3 tablespoons minced ginger

3 tablespoons minced garlic

2 tablespoons lemon juice or vinegar

1 tablespoon grated palm sugar or brown sugar

3 ripe medium tomatoes, finely chopped

1 teaspoon curry powder, or more to taste

1 teaspoon ground red pepper

$1/2$ teaspoon freshly ground black pepper

$1^1/4$ teaspoons salt

2 tablespoons finely chopped coriander leaves (cilantro)

1 Heat the oil and fry the onions until golden brown, 5–10 minutes.

2 Stir in the remaining ingredients except for the shrimp and coriander leaves and continue cooking over low heat until the oil separates.

3 Add the shrimp and stir to mix well. Cover and leave to simmer until the shrimp are cooked through, about 10 minutes.

4 Garnish with the chopped coriander leaves and serve.

Ground red pepper is a pungent red powder made from ground dried chili peppers, also known as cayenne pepper. Substitute dried red chili flakes or chili paste.

Palm Sugar is made from the sap of coconut palms or the arenga sugar palm tree. Palm sugar varies in color from gold to dark brown. It is less sweet than cane sugar and has a distinct, rich flavor. Dark brown sugar, maple syrup or a mixture of sugar and molasses are good substitutes.

Serves 4
Preparation time: 30 mins
Cooking time: 20 mins

Tempeh and Tofu Shrimp

2 oz (50 g) dried bean thread noodles, optional (see note)
$1/2$ cup (125 ml) oil
2 cups (7 oz/200 g) diced tempeh (see note)
$1/2$ cake (5 oz/150 g) firm tofu, diced
3 cloves garlic, sliced
$3/4$ in (2 cm) fresh ginger, peeled and thinly sliced
$1/2$ teaspoon dried shrimp paste (*belachan*)
1 stalk lemongrass, tender inner part of bottom third only, thinly sliced
7 oz (200 g) lean tender beef, thinly sliced (optional)
7 oz (200 g) green beans, tops, tails and strings removed, then sliced diagonally
2 red finger-length chilies, deseeded and sliced (optional)
7 oz (200 g) fresh shrimp, peeled and deveined
1 teaspoon salt
1 tablespoon tamarind pulp soaked in 2 tablespoons water, mashed and strained to obtain the juice

Serves 4
Preparation time: 35 mins
Cooking time: 30 mins

1 Soak the bean thread noodles in warm water for 3 to 4 minutes to soften. Then drain and cut the noodles into lengths. Set aside.

2 Heat the oil in a wok over medium to high heat until quite hot, then slide half the tempeh into the oil gently and cook until golden brown, about 3 to 4 minutes. Stir frequently to keep the tempeh from sticking. Remove from the oil and drain on paper towels. Repeat with the remaining tempeh. Then cook the tofu in the same way. Add more oil if necessary.

3 Drain all but 2 tablespoons of the oil from the wok. Heat the oil over medium heat, add the garlic and ginger, and stir-fry for 10 seconds. Add the *belachan* and stir-fry until the garlic is light brown, about 1 minute.

4 Add the lemongrass and beef, if using, and stir-fry for 5 minutes until the beef is lightly browned. Add the green beans, chilies and shrimp, and stir-fry for 3 minutes until the shrimp are cooked. Add the fried tempeh and tofu, and mix well.

5 Add the bean thread noodles and season with the salt. Stir-fry until the beans are just tender, about 2 minutes. Add the tamarind juice and stir to mix well. Serve with rice.

Bean thread noodles, also known as "cellophane" or "glass" noodles, are thin, clear strands made from mung bean starch and water. Soak in hot water for 15 minutes to soften. Available from Asian food stores.

Tempeh (fermented soybean cakes) are made of compressed, lightly fermented soybeans with a delicious nutty flavor. They are a rich source of protein, calcium and iron, and are low in cholesterol and sodium. Look for them in the refrigerator or freezer sections in supermarkets.

Shrimp Curry

1 1/2 lbs (700 g) jumbo shrimp, shelled, cleaned and
  deveined
1 tablespoon ground chili
2 tablespoons fish curry powder
1/2 teaspoon ground turmeric
1 in (2 1/2 cm) fresh ginger, peeled and cut into strips
2 cloves garlic, pounded
3 tablespoons oil
1/2 teaspoon mustard seeds
1 teaspoon cumin seeds
1 onion, thinly sliced
2 sprigs curry leaves (see note)
1 cup (250 ml) thick coconut milk
2 small cucumbers, deseeded and cubed
2 green finger-length chilies, cut into lengths
1 tablespoon white vinegar or lime juice
Salt to taste

1 In a bowl, combine the shrimp, chili, curry and
turmeric powders, ginger and garlic. Set aside for
5 minutes to marinate.
2 Heat the oil in a wok or skillet and stir-fry the
mustard and cumin seeds over medium heat until
aromatic, about 5 minutes. Add the onion and curry
leaves and stir-fry until the onion is golden brown,
about 4 minutes. Add the shrimp and stir-fry a
further 4 minutes.
3 Add the coconut milk, cucumber, chilies and vinegar. Bring to a boil, and simmer gently, stirring
continuously for 3 minutes. Add salt to taste and
serve hot with rice.

Curry leaves comprise sprigs of 8–15, dark green
leaves and are used to flavor Indian curries. Fresh
curry leaves should be used within a few days of purchase. Dried curry leaves keep well if stored in a dry
place. There is no good substitute. Curry leaves are
available in wet markets.

Serves 4
Preparation time: 10 mins
Cooking time: 10 mins

Lemongrass Mussels

1 lb (500 g) fresh mussels, cleaned
$^1/_2$ cup (125 ml) water
2 shallots, diced
1 stalk lemongrass, tender inner part of bottom third only, crushed and cut into lengths
$^1/_2$ teaspoon salt
$^1/_4$ teaspoon freshly ground black pepper
$^1/_2$ cup ($^1/_3$ oz/10 g) Asian basil leaves (see note)

Dipping Sauce
2 cloves garlic
2 fresh coriander roots
2 or 3 red finger-length chilies
$^1/_2$ cup (125 ml) water
$^1/_2$ cup (125 ml) fresh lime or lemon juice
$^1/_4$ cup (60 ml) fish sauce
1 teaspoon salt
1 tablespoon sugar
2 tablespoons fresh coriander leaves (cilantro), chopped

1 To prepare the Dipping Sauce, use a pestle and mortar to pound the garlic, coriander roots, and chilies until smooth. Combine this paste with the remaining Dipping Sauce ingredients in a mixing bowl and stir well.

2 Discard any open mussels. Place the remainder in a wok and add the remaining ingredients. Cover and bring to a boil over high heat, cooking for 5 minutes. Remove from the heat and serve with the Dipping Sauce. To eat, remove the mussels from the shells and dip in the Sauce.

Asian basil has pointed dark green leaves and a strong anise aroma and taste. Fresh basil leaves are used to garnish dishes. Substitute fresh Italian basil if you cannot get Asian basil.

Serves 4 to 6
Preparation time: **15 mins**
Assembling time: **5 mins**

Mixed Seafood with Vegetables

8 oz (250 g) fresh squid
1 carrot, peeled and
 sliced
8 oz (250 g) fresh
 shrimp, shelled
 and deveined, or
 sea scallops
1 cup (4 oz/100 g) broc-
 coli, cut into florets
6 oz (170 g) green
 beans, tops, tails, and
 strings removed
2 tablespoons oil
1 onion, finely sliced
4 cloves garlic, minced
1 red finger-length chili,
 sliced diagonally

Sauce
2 tablespoons soy sauce
3 tablespoons rice wine
1–2 teaspoons sugar
1 tablespoon sesame oil
$1^1/_2$ teaspoons corn-
 starch dissolved in
 $^1/_2$ cup (125 ml) water

1 To clean the squid, remove the tentacles from the body and cut out the hard beaky portion. Remove the skin from the body of the squid, and clean inside, then cut into bite-sized pieces. Dry thoroughly. Clean the cuttlefish and sea cucumber. Next, slice open the squid, cuttlefish, and sea cucumber lengthwise and cut in half. Cut each piece into strips about $^1/_4$ in ($^1/_2$ cm) wide, place them in a bowl, and set aside.

2 Cut the carrot in half lengthwise, then slice each half into pieces $^1/_4$ in ($^1/_2$ cm) wide.

3 Bring a large pot of water to a rolling boil, then blanch all the vegetables for 3 minutes. Drain and set aside.

4 To make the Sauce, combine all the ingredients and blend well. Set aside.

5 Heat the oil in a wok over high heat until smoking. Add the onions, garlic, and chili and stir-fry to release their aromas, about 1 minute.

6 Add the seafood and vegetables and continue to stir-fry until all the ingredients are well coated with oil, about 2 minutes.

7 Stir the Sauce to mix, then add to the wok and continue to stir-fry until the Sauce is well blended with seafood and vegetables, for 2 to 3 minutes. Remove from the heat, transfer to a platter, and serve.

Serves 4
Preparation time: **25 mins**
Cooking time: **10 mins**

Garlic Squid

This type of dish belongs to a category of home-style Sichuan cooking known as *xiao chao*, which literally means "small fry." Squid has long been prized in Chinese family kitchens as an excellent yet inexpensive nutritional source of protein and essential minerals from the sea.

1 lb (500 g) fresh squid
1 tablespoon oil
5 to 6 cloves garlic, thinly sliced
4 slices fresh ginger
2 red finger-length chilies, cut into pieces
3 green onions (scallions), washed and cut into pieces
2 stalks fresh celery, strings removed, washed and cut into pieces
Salt to taste

Sauce
2 teaspoons rice wine
1 teaspoon sugar
1 tablespoon sesame oil
1 tablespoon sweet dark soy sauce (see note)
1 tablespoon water

1 Combine the Sauce ingredients and set aside.
2 Remove the tentacles from the squid and cut out the hard beaky portion. Remove the skin from the body of the squid, and clean inside, then cut into bite-sized pieces. Dry thoroughly and set aside.
3 Heat the remaining oil in a wok over medium heat, add the garlic, ginger, and chilies, and stir-fry for about 2 minutes.
4 Increase the heat to high, add the green onions, celery, and squid, and stir-fry for 1 minute. Add the Sauce mixture and continue to stir-fry for 3 to 4 minutes more. Remove to a platter and serve.

If **sweet dark soy sauce** is not available, add $1/2$ tablespoon brown sugar to 1 tablespoon regular soy sauce.

Serves 4
Preparation time: **15 mins + 2–3 hours soaking**
Cooking time: **15 mins**

Sichuan Squid with Dried Chilies

Gung bao dishes are attributed to the private kitchen of a certain Duke of Bao in ancient Sichuan, whose personal chef was the reigning master of gourmet cuisine in his time. It involves first scorching dried red chilies in searing hot oil until they are almost black, then tossing in the main ingredients to "explode-fry" (*bao chao*) them quickly in pungent hot oil, and finishing it all off with a savory sauce. This recipe works equally well with chicken chunks or shrimp.

1 whole squid, about 1 lb (500 g)
3 tablespoons oil
5 dried red chilies, cut across in thirds
10 Sichuan peppercorns
3 slices fresh ginger, cut in thirds
2 green onions (scallions), cut in thirds

Sauce
1 tablespoon soy sauce
$^1/_2$ to 1 tablespoon sugar
1 tablespoon rice wine
1 teaspoon tomato ketchup
2 teaspoons vinegar
2 teaspoons sesame oil
2 teaspoons cornstarch dissolved in $^1/_2$ cup (125 ml) water

Serves 4
Preparation time: **10 mins**
Cooking time: **10 mins**

1 Lay the squid flat on a cutting board, and with a sharp knife, make diagonal cuts across the entire surface, cutting only about halfway into the flesh. Repeat the same pattern at a 90-degree angle to the first cuts making cross-hatch marks $^1/_2$ inch (1 cm) apart. Then cut the squid into 1 in ($2^1/_2$ cm) square or rectangular pieces.

2 To make the Sauce, combine the Sauce ingredients and set aside.

3 Heat the oil in a wok over high heat until very hot. Add the chilies and scorch for 30 to 60 seconds, then add the Sichuan peppercorns, ginger, and green onions, and stir-fry swiftly to release the aromas, about 1 minute.

4 Add the drained squid to the wok and stir-fry for 30 to 60 seconds, then stir the Sauce mixture to mix the ingredients and add to the squid. Stir-fry to blend all flavors for about 3 more minutes, then remove to a platter and serve.

If you like the sharp fresh flavor of coriander leaves, sprinkle some, chopped, onto the finished dish. You may also prepare this recipe with cuttlefish or scallops. The best type of dried chilies for this dish is the medium or large size, which are highly aromatic but not too hot. The smaller the chili, the fiercer its flavor.

Five Spice Chicken

You can also add $1/2$ cup (60 g) fresh or frozen green peas after stir-frying the chicken for a minute or two. A sprinkling of chopped fresh coriander leaves (cilantro) on the finished dish goes very well with these flavors.

12 oz (350 g) boneless
  chicken meat, cubed
3 tablespoons sesame oil
5 to 6 cloves garlic,
  minced
2 green onions (scal-
  lions), cut into pieces

Marinade
2 tablespoons rice wine
1 tablespoon soy sauce
1 teaspoon sesame oil
1 teaspoon sugar
$1/2$ teaspoon salt
2 teaspoons five spice
  powder
1 teaspoon cornstarch
  dissolved in 1 table-
  spoon water

1 Place the chicken in a bowl with the Marinade ingredients, stirring to coat the chicken well. Set aside for 15 to 20 minutes.

2 Drain the Marinade, reserving all the liquid.

3 Heat the sesame oil over high heat, and when hot, add the garlic and chicken, and stir-fry for 3 to 4 minutes, then add the reserved Marinade and green onions and cook for another 2 minutes. Transfer to a serving dish.

Five Spice Powder is a highly aromatic blend of Sichuan pepper, cinnamon, clove, fennel and star anise, ground to a fine powder and used to season stir-fried foods, in marinades and for sauces.

Serves 4
Preparation time: **20 mins**
Cooking time: **6 mins**

Yogurt Chicken Curry

- 1 chicken, skinned and cut into serving pieces
- 1 teaspoon ground red pepper
- 1 teaspoon salt
- 1 cup (250 ml) plain yogurt
- 2 tablespoons oil
- 3 onions, finely chopped
- 2 tablespoons minced ginger
- 2 tablespoons minced garlic
- 2 green finger-length chilies (more if desired), finely chopped
- 2 tablespoons ground coriander
- 1 teaspoon ground cumin
- 4 cups (7 oz/200 g) finely chopped fresh coriander leaves (cilantro)
- 2$\frac{1}{2}$ cups (4 oz/100 g) mint leaves, washed and finely chopped

1 Mix the chicken pieces with the chili powder, salt and half of the yogurt. Marinate for 15 minutes. (Reserve the remainder of the yogurt for later use.)
2 In a large saucepan or wok, heat the oil over medium heat and stir-fry the onions until transparent before adding the minced ginger and garlic. Stir-fry until fragrant, about 5 minutes. Add the green chilies, coriander and cumin powders, stirring well into the onion mixture.
3 Drain the chicken pieces and add to the pan. Increase the heat to high and stir-fry for 5 minutes. Stir constantly to prevent sticking and burning.
4 Scrape the leftover marinade from the bowl into the cooking chicken pieces, and add the remaining yogurt. Add the chopped coriander and mint leaves and mix well.
5 Bring to a boil, then cover with a lid, reduce the heat to low and cook until the chicken pieces are done, about 20 to 25 minutes. Serve hot.

Ground red pepper is a pungent red powder made from ground dried chili peppers, also known as cayenne pepper. Substitute dried red chili flakes or chili paste.

Serves 4–6
Preparation time: 20 mins
Cooking time: 25 mins

Sichuan Chicken with Dried Chilies

If you don't like biting into the whole Sichuan peppercorns, omit them and sprinkle the finished dish with Sichuan Pepper-Salt Powder instead. If sweet dark soy sauce is not available, substitute with 3 tablespoons regular soy sauce mixed with 2 teaspoons sugar.

1 lb (500 g) boneless chicken meat, cubed
2 tablespoons oil
3–4 dried red chilies, deseeded and cut into thirds
8 Sichuan peppercorns
3 cloves garlic, coarsely chopped
6 slices fresh ginger
3 green onions (scallions), cut into pieces

Marinade
1 tablespoon rice wine
1 teaspoon soy sauce
1 teaspoon sesame oil
$1/2$ teaspoon sugar, or more to taste
$1/2$ teaspoon cornstarch dissolved in 4 tablespoons water

Sauce
3 tablespoons soy sauce
1 teaspoon vinegar
1 tablespoon rice wine
1 teaspoon sesame oil
1 teaspoon salt
1 teaspoon cornstarch dissolved in 4 tablespoons water
2 teaspoons sugar, or more to taste

1 Place the chicken chunks in a bowl and cover with the Marinade ingredients. Mix well and set aside for 15 to 20 minutes.
2 Combine the Sauce ingredients and set aside.
3 Heat the oil in a wok over high heat until hot, add the dried chilies, and scorch for 30 to 60 seconds. Add the Sichuan peppercorns, garlic and ginger, and stir-fry for 30 seconds more.
4 Add the marinated chicken and stir-fry, until the chicken changes color and firms, about 4 minutes. Add the Sauce, stir to blend all the ingredients, cover, reduce the heat to medium, and braise for 5 minutes. Remove the lid, add the green onions, stir to mix with the chicken for 30 seconds, then remove to a serving dish.

To make **Sichuan Pepper-Salt Powder**, dry-toast 2 tablespoons Sichuan peppercorns with $1/2$ teaspoon salt in a dry pan, then grind to a fine powder.

Serves 4
Preparation time: **30 mins**
Cooking time: **15 mins**

Turmeric Chicken

1 chicken, cut into serving pieces

$1^1/_4$ in (3 cm) fresh turmeric root, peeled, sliced and ground, or $1^1/_4$ teaspoons ground turmeric

$1^1/_2$–2 teaspoons salt

$^1/_2$ teaspoon freshly ground black pepper

$^1/_2$ cup (125 ml) oil

1 teaspoon sugar

1 onion, cut into rings

Serves 4
Preparation time: 30 mins
Cooking time: 25 mins

1 Rinse and pat the chicken dry with paper towels.

2 Combine the ground turmeric, salt and pepper in a small bowl. Rub this mixture into the chicken and set aside to marinate for at least 20 minutes.

3 Heat the oil in a wok over high heat until very hot, slide the marinated chicken pieces into the hot oil gently using a spatula, and stir-fry the chicken until it browns slightly and the juices are sealed in, about 4 minutes. Reduce the heat to medium and continue to stir-fry the chicken for 10 minutes.

4 Add the sugar and onion, and stir-fry until the onion is lightly browned and the chicken is cooked, about 8 to 10 minutes. Remove from the oil and drain on paper towels. Serve hot.

Thai Chicken with Basil

2 tablespoons oil
3 cloves garlic, minced
2 bird's-eye chilies, sliced
2 tablespoons fresh green peppercorns (optional)
10 oz (300 g) fresh chicken meat, cut into thin strips
4 oz (120 g) baby corn
8 dried black Chinese mushrooms, soaked in warm
    water for 20 minutes, stems discarded and caps sliced
$2/_3$ cup (4 oz/100 g) green beans, tops and tails
    removed, cut into lengths
$1^1/_4$ cups (4 oz/125 g) cauliflower florets
2 red finger-length chilies, thinly sliced diagonally
1 tablespoon fish sauce
1 tablespoon oyster sauce
1 tablespoon sugar
$1/_2$ teaspoon freshly ground black pepper
$1/_2$ cup (125 ml) chicken stock
2 sprigs Thai basil leaves

1 Heat the oil in a wok or skillet over high heat. Add the garlic, bird's-eye chilies and green peppercorns. Stir-fry until the garlic turns golden brown and fragrant.
2 Add the chicken, baby corn, mushrooms, green beans, cauliflower and chilies, and stir-fry for about 5 minutes until the chicken is cooked and the vegetables are tender. Then season with the fish sauce, oyster sauce, sugar and black pepper. Mix well and add the chicken stock. Stir-fry for a further minute, add the basil leaves and remove from heat.
3 Serve hot with steamed rice.

Thai basil (*horapa*) tastes rather like Italian sweet basil with a hint of anise and is used in red and green curries as well as salads and stir-fries. It is available year round. If you cannot find it, use Italian basil.

Serves 4
Preparation time: **10 mins**
Cooking time: **10 mins**

Cumin Chicken

1 chicken, cut into serving pieces
1 teaspoon salt
$1/4$ teaspoon ground white pepper
1 tablespoon cumin seeds
$1/2$ tablespoon fennel seeds
1 teaspoon black peppercorns
$3/4$ in (2 cm) fresh ginger, peeled and sliced
5 cloves garlic, peeled
3 tablespoons oil
1 cup (250 ml) water

1 Place the chicken in a bowl. Sprinkle it with salt and pepper, and set aside.
2 Dry-fry the cumin, fennel and black peppercorns over low heat in a skillet until fragrant, about 2 minutes. Set aside to cool slightly, then grind to a powder in a mortar or grinder. Grind or crush the ginger and garlic to a smooth paste and set aside.
3 Heat the oil in a wok over medium heat and stir-fry the minced ginger and garlic for 30 seconds. Add the chicken and stir-fry for 10 minutes until browned.
4 Add the ground spices and stir-fry for another 10 minutes. Then add the water and bring to a boil, scraping the bottom of the pan to loosen any spices that may be stuck to it.
5 Reduce the heat and simmer, uncovered, stirring frequently, until the chicken is tender and most of the liquid has evaporated, about 12 to 15 minutes. Serve garnished with thinly sliced green onions and chilies (see photo) if desired.

For a healthier alternative, remove the chicken skin and fat before cooking.

Serves 4
Preparation time: **20 mins**
Cooking time: **35 mins**

Spicy Indian Chicken

3 chicken breasts
3 green finger-length
  chilies, chopped
4 cloves garlic
3/4 in (2 cm) fresh
  ginger
2 onions, diced
1 tablespoon vinegar or
  lime juice
2 tablespoons oil
1 teaspoon cumin seeds
1 teaspoon fennel seeds
3 tablespoons ground
  cumin
1 teaspoon salt
1 tablespoon freshly
  ground black pepper

1 Skin and thinly slice the chicken breasts, and set aside.
2 Grind the green chilies, garlic, ginger, onions and vinegar to a paste in a blender. In a large bowl, stir the paste into the shredded chicken and leave to marinate in the refrigerator for an hour or so.
2 Heat the oil in a wok and stir-fry the cumin and fennel seeds until aromatic. Add in the marinated chicken pieces along with the marinade. Stir in the cumin powder, salt and pepper and mix well, continuing to cook until the chicken is done and fairly dry.

Serves 4
Preparation time: **15 mins**
Cooking time: **20 mins**

Spicy Indian Pork

1 1/2 lbs (700 g) pork
  loin
2 tablespoons oil
1 teaspoon fennel
  seeds, slightly crushed
1 teaspoon cumin seeds
2 onions, diced
4 dried red chilies,
  cut into pieces
2 tomatoes, thinly sliced
2 cloves garlic, minced
2 green finger-length
  chilies, sliced
2 teaspoons ground red
  pepper (page 10)
1 tablespoon vinegar
1 teaspoon salt

1 Cut the pork into bite-sized cubes and set aside.

2 Heat the oil in a wok or skillet and stir-fry the fennel and cumin seeds until aromatic, then add the onions and stir-fry until golden brown, about 10 minutes in total.

3 Add the chilies, sliced tomato, ginger and garlic and stir-fry over low heat until the oil separates. Add the rest of the ingredients except the vinegar and cook until the pork is tender, about 20 minutes.

4 Just before removing from the heat, add the vinegar, mix well and serve.

Serves 4
Preparation time: 15 mins
Cooking time: 40 mins

Sweet Soy Pork with Orange Peel

You'll find this dish served in almost all Chinese night markets. Home cooks pride themselves on creating their own original blend of seasonings for this dish, which is one of the richest on the entire Chinese menu. Chopped fresh coriander leaves (cilantro) makes an excellent garnish for braised pork shank, because its sharp, fresh taste balances nicely with the rich, sweet flavors of the pork. You may reserve the remaining braising sauce in a jar in the refrigerator and use it as a flavoring sauce for stir-fry cooking, or to braise other foods, such as tofu or fish.

1 whole pork shank, about 3 lbs (1$^1/_2$ kgs)
1 cup (250 ml) soy sauce
2 cups (500 ml) rice wine
2 cups (500 ml) water
$^1/_2$ cup (125 ml) vinegar
$^1/_2$ cup (3 oz/75 g) sugar, preferably rock sugar
2 in (5 cm) ginger, sliced
6 green onions (scallions), cut into sections
Peel of one whole fresh orange
1 stick cinnamon, broken into 2 or 3 pieces
1 teaspoon Sichuan peppercorns
2 whole star anise (see note)
8 oz (250 g) fresh spinach, blanched

Serves 4
Preparation time: 15 mins
Cooking time: 3 hours

1 Fill a large stockpot about two-thirds full of water and bring to a rolling boil. Place the pork shank into the water and bring to a boil, then pour all the water out into the sink, leaving the shank in the pot.

2 Add the remaining ingredients except the spinach to the pot and place the pot on high heat and bring the contents to a boil, then reduce the heat to medium, cover with a lid and simmer for about 3 hours, turning the shank over occasionally. After 2 hours, reduce heat to medium–low, and check from time to time to make sure that the sauce has not evaporated too much. If the level of sauce does not cover at least one-third of the shank, add another cup or two of rice wine mixed in equal portions with water

3 When done, turn off the heat, and let the pot stand, covered, on stove until ready to serve.

4 To serve, lay a bed of blanched spinach on a platter, then transfer the whole shank onto the spinach. Use a knife and fork to break the shank apart, then drizzle some of the braising sauce over it.

Star anise is a dark brown, strongly-flavored spice that resembles an eight-pointed star. Its aroma is similar to anise or cinnamon. Store in a tightly-sealed jar in a cool, dry place.

Tangy Tamarind Pork

3 tablespoons oil plus
2 cups (500 ml) for
deep-frying
1 onion, diced
3 cloves garlic, minced
2 teaspoons yellow bean
paste
2 tablespoons tomato
paste
$1/4$ cup (2 oz/50 g)
sugar
$1/4$ cup (60 ml) fish sauce
2 tablespoons tamarind
pulp soaked in $1/4$ cup
(60 ml) water, mashed
and strained to obtain
the juice
Juice of 1 lemon
Grated rind of 1 lemon
1 cup (5 oz/150 g) lean
pork loin, thinly sliced
1 lb (500 g) dried rice
vermicelli (*beehoon* or
mifen), soaked for 5
minutes and drained
1 cup ($1^1/_3$ oz/40 g)
garlic chives (*gu cai*)
or 2 green onions
(scallions), cut into
lengths
8 oz (250 g) bean
sprouts (optional)
Lemon wedges, to serve

1 Heat 3 tablespoons of oil in a wok over medium-high heat. Stir-fry the onion, garlic, yellow bean paste, and tomato paste until fragrant, about 3 minutes.
2 Add the sugar, fish sauce, and tamarind juice, and bring to a boil. Stir in the lemon juice, lemon rind, and pork. Reduce the heat to low and cook uncovered for about 30 minutes, stirring occasionally.
3 Meanwhile, heat the 2 cups (500 ml) of oil in a large saucepan over medium-high heat. Add the noodles, one handful at a time, to the oil in a single layer. Fry one side until golden and carefully turn the layer of noodles over to fry the other side. Remove the noodles and drain them on paper towels. Repeat until all the noodles are fried.
4 Arrange the fried noodles on a serving platter, ladle the meat and sauce over them, and garnish with the garlic chives. Surround the noodles with the bean sprouts and garnish with the lemon wedges, if desired. Serve hot.

Serves 4 to 6
Preparation time: **10 mins**
Cooking time: **40 mins**

Chili Beef Steaks

1 1/3 lbs (600 g) beef sirloin or topside, cut into large chunks
5 dried chilies, deseeded and cut into lengths
2 red finger-length chilies, deseeded and sliced
6 shallots, peeled
2 cloves garlic, peeled
1/2 cup (125 ml) oil
2 onions, sliced into rings
3/4 in (2 cm) ginger, peeled and shredded
2 teaspoons sugar
1 teaspoon salt
1 tablespoon lime juice

Serves 4
Preparation time: 20 mins
Cooking time: 1 1/2 to 2 hours

1 Place the beef in a pan, add enough water to cover it and bring to a boil. Skim off any foam that rises. Reduce the heat, cover and simmer until the beef is very tender, about 1 1/4 to 1 1/2 hours.

2 Soak the dried chilies in warm water for 10 to 15 minutes to soften. Then deseed and drain. Grind the drained chilies, fresh chilies, shallots and garlic to a smooth paste in a mortar or blender, adding a little oil if necessary to keep the blades turning.

3 When the beef is ready, drain and set aside to cool, reserving the beef stock for other dishes. When cool enough to handle, cut the beef into thin slices.

4 Heat 4 tablespoons of the oil in a wok over very high heat and briskly stir-fry half the beef until lightly browned, about 2 minutes. Remove from the oil and drain on paper towels. Repeat with the rest of the beef. Set aside.

5 Reduce the heat to medium and stir-fry the onions until translucent, about 2 minutes. Remove from the oil and drain on paper towels. Add the ginger to the wok and stir-fry until golden brown, about 1 minute. Remove from the oil and drain on paper towels.

6 Reduce the heat to low, add the remaining oil and stir-fry the ground paste until the oil separates from the mixture, about 5 to 6 minutes.

7 Return the beef, onions and ginger to the wok and season with the salt, sugar and lime juice. Increase the heat to medium and stir-fry until the beef is coated with the paste, about 1 to 2 minutes. Serve.

Vietnamese Beef Stew

This dish always wins much praise, and may become your favorite way to serve beef stew. This works well served with rice, pasta or French bread.

1 1/2 lbs (700 g) beef, cubed
2 tablespoons oil
1 large onion, diced
4 cloves garlic
3 cups (750 ml) water
4 tablespoons tomato paste
2 star anise (see note)
1 large carrot, cut into chunks
2 potatoes, cut into chunks
1 daikon radish (about 12 oz/350 g), peeled and cut into chunks

Marinade
2 stalks lemongrass, tender inner part of bottom third only, minced
1 red finger-length chili, deseeded and diced
2 tablespoons minced fresh ginger root
1 teaspoon ground cinnamon
1 teaspoon curry powder
2 tablespoons fish sauce
1 teaspoon salt
1/4 teaspoon freshly ground black pepper

1 Make the Marinade first by combining all the ingredients in a large bowl and mixing well. Place the beef cubes in the Marinade and mix until well coated. Allow to marinate for at least 30 minutes.

2 Heat the oil in a wok or large saucepan over high heat and stir-fry the onion and garlic until fragrant, 30 seconds to 1 minute. Add the marinated beef and the Marinade and stir-fry for about 3 minutes, until the beef is browned on all sides. Add the water, tomato paste and star anise, and bring the mixture to a boil. Reduce the heat to low and simmer uncovered for about 1 hour. Add the vegetables and continue to simmer for another 20 minutes, until the beef is tender and the vegetables are cooked. Remove from the heat, transfer to a serving bowl and serve with steamed rice.

Star anise is a dark brown, strongly-flavored spice that resembles an eight-pointed star. Its aroma is similar to anise or cinnamon. Store in a tightly-sealed jar in a cool, dry place.

Serves 6 to 8
Preparation time: 20 mins + 30 mins to marinate
Cooking time: 1 hour 25 mins

Beef with Bamboo Shoots

3 tablespoons oil
1 lb (500 g) beef sirloin, thinly sliced
3 cloves garlic, minced
3 green onions (scallions), cut into lengths
8 oz (250 g) canned or pre-cooked bamboo shoots, drained and thinly sliced (see note)
1 tablespoon fish sauce
1 tablespoon oyster sauce
$1/4$ teaspoon salt
$1/4$ teaspoon freshly ground black pepper
4 tablespoons sesame seeds, dry-roasted in a skillet for 10 minutes over low heat

1 Heat 2 tablespoons of the oil in a wok or skillet over high heat. Stir-fry the beef for about 1 minute, until it changes color. Remove from the heat and set aside.
2 Heat the remaining oil in the wok or skillet, stir-fry the garlic, green onion and bamboo shoot for 2 to 3 minutes, seasoning with the fish sauce, oyster sauce, salt and pepper. Return the beef to the skillet, add the sesame seeds and stir-fry for 3 more minutes, until the beef is tender and cooked. Remove from the heat.
3 Transfer to a serving platter and serve hot with steamed rice.

Bamboo shoots, are the fresh shoots of the bamboo plant. Pre-cooked bamboo shoots, packed in water, can be found in the refrigerated section of supermarkets. Canned bamboo shoots are also pre-cooked but should be boiled for 5 minutes to refresh before using.

Serves 4
Preparation time: **10 mins**   Cooking time: **10 mins**

Thai Red Curry Beef

3/4 cup (185 ml) thick coconut milk

2 tablespoons Red Curry Paste (page 7)

1 lb (500 g) beef tenderloin, sliced

1 1/2 cups (5 oz/150 g) eggplant, cut into chunks

1 1/2 tablespoons fresh green peppercorns or 1/2 tablespoon black peppercorns

1 cup (5 oz/150 g) green beans, sliced diagonally

4 tablespoons fish sauce

3 teaspoons sugar

1/3 cup (80 ml) chicken stock

8 kaffir lime leaves, torn into pieces (see note)

Basil leaves, to garnish

2 red finger-length chilies, sliced, to garnish

Serves 4

Preparation time: **20 mins**

Cooking time: **25 mins**

1 Heat the thick coconut milk in a wok or skillet over medium heat for about 2 minutes. Stir in the Red Curry Paste and simmer until the mixture has thickened and reduced to one-third, about 10 minutes.

2 Add the beef and stir-fry until cooked. Add the eggplant, peppercorns and green beans. Stir-fry for another minute until the vegetables are tender, then season with the fish sauce, sugar, chicken stock and lime leaves. Mix well before removing from heat.

3 Serve hot, garnished with the basil leaves and chilies.

Kaffir lime leaves are the fragrant leaves of the kaffir lime plant. The leaves are used whole in soups and curries, or shredded finely and added to salads.

Beef with Bean Sprouts

1 teaspoon rice wine
1 teaspoon soy sauce
1 teaspoon sugar
$1/4$ teaspoon ground
   white pepper
$1/4$ cup (60 ml) water
1 teaspoon cornstarch
5 oz (150 g) fillet steak,
   shredded
4 tablespoons olive oil
2 shallots, thinly sliced
2 cloves garlic, thinly
   sliced
8 oz (250 g) bean
   sprouts, tails removed
2 red finger-length
   chilies, deseeded and
   thinly sliced
1 teaspoon sherry
2 tablespoons chicken
   stock
1 tablespoon oyster sauce
1 teaspoon soy sauce
$1/2$ teaspoon sugar
$1/4$ teaspoon ground
   white pepper
1 teaspoon cornstarch
   stirred into 1 table-
   spoon water
1 teaspoon sesame oil
1 green onion (scallion),
   thinly sliced

1 Measure the rice wine, soy sauce, sugar, pepper, water, and cornstarch into a medium bowl and stir in the shredded beef. Set aside for 30 minutes to 1 hour, then blend in 2 tablespoons of the oil and continue to marinate for another 15 to 30 minutes.

2 Heat 1 tablespoon of the remaining oil in a wok or skillet and fry the shredded beef on high heat for 2 minutes or until partially cooked. Set aside.

3 In a clean wok, heat the remaining 1 tablespoon of oil; toss in the shallots and garlic and fry until fragrant. Stir-fry the bean sprouts over high heat for about 8 seconds, then pour in the beef and add the chilies. Stir-fry briskly, then sizzle in the wine, add the stock and season with the oyster sauce, soy sauce, sugar, and pepper.

4 Stir the cornstarch mixture and add it to the skillet. Toss in the green onion and sprinkle with the sesame oil. Serve hot.

Serves 2
Preparation time: **15 mins + 45 mins standing**
Cooking time: **10 mins**

Sichuan Lamb or Pork

Instead of green onions (scallions) you can also use finely sliced onions or bean sprouts as a bed for the cooked lamb. If using pork, increase the cooking time to 6 minutes for the pre-cooking, and 6 minutes for the final cooking. This is also an excellent way to prepare venison, wild boar, and other wild game meats.

1 1/2 lbs (700 g) lamb loin
4 green onions (scallions), cut in half and into thin strips
3 tablespoons oil

Marinade
1 teaspoon cornstarch dissolved in 1 tablespoon of water
1 tablespoon soy sauce
1 egg white
1/2 teaspoon sugar

Sauce
1 tablespoon yellow bean paste
1 teaspoon sugar, or more to taste
1 teaspoon salt
2 teaspoons rice wine
1 tablespoon ground Sichuan pepper
1 tablespoon sesame oil
1 tablespoon bottled chili sauce

1 Cut the lamb into thin slices and place in a bowl.
2 To make the Marinade, combine the ingredients, then pour over the lamb and set aside for 15 minutes.
3 Spread the shredded green onions evenly onto a serving plate and set aside.
4 Combine the Sauce ingredients and set aside.
5 Heat 2 tablespoons of oil in a wok over high heat until hot. Add the marinated lamb and stir-fry for about 4 minutes. Remove the lamb to a plate and set aside. Discard the oil.
6 Heat the remaining 1 tablespoon of oil in the wok and when hot, add the Sauce mixture and stir-fry for about 1 minute.
7 Return the lamb to the wok and cook for another 3 to 4 minutes. Remove the lamb and place on top of the shredded green onions on the serving dish.

Serves 4
Preparation time: 15 mins
Cooking time: 10 mins

Indian Lamb with Cashews

1 1/2 lbs (700 g) lamb
4 tablespoons oil
2 cinnamon sticks
6 cardamom pods
6 cloves
1 teaspoon fennel seeds
1 onion, peeled and
   sliced
2 ripe tomatoes, diced
1 1/2 tablespoons meat
   curry powder
1 tablespoon ground
   coriander
2 cups (500 ml) water
1 teaspoon salt
100g (1/2 cup) dry roast-
   ed unsalted cashew
   nuts, to garnish

Spice Paste
2 onions, sliced
1 in (2 1/2 cm) ginger
2 cloves garlic
1 teaspoon black pepper-
   corns
2 sprigs curry leaves,
   removed from stalk
3 dried red chilies, cut
   into lengths
1/2 cup (20 g) mint leaves
1/2 cup (25 g) fresh
   coriander leaves
   (cilantro)

1 Cut the lamb into bite-sized cubes and set aside.

2 Grind the Spice Paste ingredients in a blender until fine. Set aside.

3 Heat the oil in a wok over medium heat and fry the cinnamon, cardamoms, cloves and fennel until aromatic. Add the onion and tomatoes and stir-fry until the onion turns golden brown, about 3 minutes.

4 Stir in the ground Spice Paste, the meat curry powder, *garam masala* and coriander powder. Add the water and mutton or lamb. Cook until the meat is tender and the liquid evaporates, about 30 minutes. Season with salt to taste and garnish with dry roasted cashew nuts.

Serves 4
Preparation time: 40 mins
Cooking time: 33 mins

Complete Recipe Listing